Global Migra

The Health Care Implications of Immigration and Population Movements

The proceedings of the American Academy of Nursing 1995 Annual Meeting and Conference, *Health Care in Times of Global Transitions*

PAUL R. EPSTEIN, M.D., M.P.H., *Department of Medicine, Harvard Medical School*

MICHAEL HOFFMAN, J.D., *Officer, International Humanitarian Law, American Red Cross*

MI JA KIM, PH.D., R.N., F.A.A.N., *Vice Chancellor for Research and Dean, Graduate College, University of Illinois at Chicago*

JULIENE G. LIPSON, PH.D., F.A.A.N., *Professor, University of California, San Francisco*

JUDITH MAYOTTE, PHD., *Special Advisor for Refugee Issues, Bureau of Population, Rufgees, and Migration, United States Department of State*

ANGELA BARRON MCBRIDE, PH.D., R.N., F.A.A.N., *Distinguished Professor and Dean, Indiana University School of Nursing*

MARY LOU DE LEON SIANTZ, PH.D., R.N., F.A.A.N., *Associate Professor, Psychiatric-Mental Health Nursing, Indiana University School of Nursing*

ROGER P. WINTER, *Director, The U.S. Committee for Refugees*

Global Migration:
The Health Care Implications of Immigration and Population Movements

ISBN#: 1-55810-133-0
G-194/1/97

Published by:

American Academy of Nursing
600 Maryland Avenue, S.W.
Suite 100 West
Washington, DC 20024-2571

Design and editorial services provided by: C&W Creative Services

Table *of* Contents

Forward

ANGELA BARRON MCBRIDE, PhD, RN, FAAN
Distinguished Professor and Dean
Indiana University School of Nursing

It was my privilege to be President of the American Academy of Nursing at the time of the conference on Health Care in Times of Global Transition, so I would like to speak to why this was the focus in 1995. Because fellowship in the Academy cuts across clinical specialties and functional areas, each conference we hold should serve as an attempt to grapple with cutting-edge issues that bridge the usual practice divisions. Encouraged by the Academy's expert panel on international matters under the leadership of Mi Ja Kim, the Governing Council sought to emphasize the extent to which health care is increasingly a global matter not limited by national systems (or non-systems), geographic boundaries, or the guild concerns of any one profession.

As an academy, we wanted to confront our own parochial sensibilities, which too often have equated "international" with trips to foreign lands and one-way information flow, and to end with all attendees having some greater sense that their everyday lives can be either constrained or advantaged by global developments. We knew that we would count as a successful outcome each attendee who began to think more personally about NAFTA trade agreements, emerging microbes, multiracial millions, internet connections, language requirements, and Healthy People 2000 goals. Certainly, everything that was said at the conference about addressing ethnic and racial diversity had meaning internationally, but also at home in making our own communities work.

This conference served notice on emerging problems, but it also provided an occasion to think profoundly of the accomplishments of nurses in the Red Cross, WHO, and the ICN. It is increasingly said that there are only six degrees of separation between each one of us and everyone else on the planet, and the conference inspired us to start thinking about these connections.

Introduction

MI JA KIM, PH.D., R.N., F.A.A.N.
*Vice Chancellor for Research and
Dean, Graduate College
University of Illinois at Chicago*

IN THE FALL OF 1995, MEMBERS OF THE AMERICAN ACADEMY OF NURSING GATHERED in Washington D.C. at their annual meeting to examine the range of policy issues related to health care in times of global transition. Looking back, those months are remembered for the assassination of Yitzak Rabin, the very close vote in Quebec on that province's secession from Canada, and the 50th anniversary of the United Nations—all events that demonstrate the world's interconnectedness and changeability.

Academy members, as nurse leaders, take very seriously our obligation to have at least a general understanding of the impact of health on trade, migration, and international humanitarian issues. Maricel Manfredi of the Pan American Health Organization recalled for the conference the fact that health is the foundation upon which all human endeavor rests. Roger Winter, in his stirring Keynote Address, stressed the global importance of nursing's role as the major provider of health care around the world.

And what more committed group to gather to examine the subject of health care in times of global transition than the American Academy of Nursing, which is charged with the mission of "providing visionary leadership to the nursing profession and the public in shaping future health policy, advancing scientific knowledge, and in influencing the development of effective health care policies."

During this post-Cold-War time of global uncertainty and fragmentation, it is critical that nurses assume a leadership role in these discussions, and that we expand our thinking to a global plane. As Dr. McBride put it so ably in her welcoming remarks: "We, who have been traditionally knowledgeable about human development, must be prepared to expand our thinking to include global transitions, so as not to be marginalized by policies that ignore our concerns as a profession nor our commitment to those too frequently leading marginalized lives—women, children, the elderly."

One of the goals of the Academy's 1995 Annual Meeting and Conference, co-sponsored by the American Red Cross, was the compilation of a policy document. The following document addresses immigration and population movements and the implications of these movements for specific populations (women, older adults, children), emerging microbes, and ethics and human rights. It also includes strategies for policy changes and recommendations for action in nursing practice, education, and research. We hope we have succeeded in this modest mission and welcome your feedback.

This conference was a start, a very good start, by a group of learned and committed people—speakers, presenters, facilitators, rapporteurs, and attendees alike. But like the eternal dilemma that seems to confront anyone working in a profession that seeks the betterment of the human condition, it is only a start. As nurses, our professional mission requires commitment, and as nurse leaders we must and can make a difference.

As you read on, please consider how you can heed the advice of the presenters: We must think globally and act locally. The world is too small today to do otherwise.

Keynote Address

ROGER P. WINTER, DIRECTOR
The U.S. Committee for Refugees

IMMIGRANTS AND REFUGEES: THE DIFFERENCE

When we distinguish between "immigrants" and "refugees," we need to focus on some basic differences. First, the difference between a typical immigrant and a typical refugee is that the former is moving while the latter is fleeing. The things that cause people to leave their homes can be loosely divided into "push factors" and "pull factors." When people immigrate, they are often searching for opportunity, stability, growth, education for their children, and so forth. These are what we call "pull factors." Opportunity pulls people in a certain direction.

When we talk about refugees, however, we are talking about much more than being "pulled." They may not want to leave where they are, but they are being pushed by circumstances: violence, persecution, or human rights abuses. Their motivations are different from those of immigrants. When people flee as refugees, they need and deserve to be rescued.

Those of us who regularly work with refugees like to look at the issue of refugees as a humanitarian issue. However, everything about refugees, despite the humanitarian aspects to their situation, is really political—from the way individuals become refugees in the first place, to how they decide where they are going to flee, to whether the countries of the world are going to share the burden of meeting their needs. Underlying the political elements of the refugee problem is the fact that refugees are largely fleeing their governments. That is about as political a relationship as one can get, and its political nature carries through the whole of the international community's response to refugees.

Essentially, people become refugees when the normal relationship between a government and the individuals governed is ruptured. That normal relationship, in which a government protects the people living within its boundaries (and, in particular, its citizens), can be ruptured because the government becomes an abuser of the population. That is more often than not the crux of what precipitates a refugee movement.

SOVEREIGN NATION STATES: THE HISTORICAL CONTEXT

To understand the situation today, we need to look at yesterday for context, background, and history. The world is comprised of approximately 200 sovereign nation-states. Sovereign nation-states, as a construct of human society, are relatively new in historical their allegiances—such as tribes, races, religions, and clans—have deeper roots in human history than does the modern nation-state.

Most of today's states arose from the ruins of collapsing empires; the British Empire, the European colonies, the Ottoman Empire, and many others. When empires collapsed, they often left behind the framework and the borders of the states that exist today. The delineation of many of those states' borders was socially artificial: when a group was constructing an empire, its members did not usually worry too much about the social sensibilities of the population(s) they were subjugating. When empires dissolved, they left behind a patchwork of states of varying historical and popular legitimacy. These were often fairly incoherent states with little potential for long-term viability. Commonly, these are the states producing significant numbers of refugees today. Not only are there states that do not necessarily cater to the needs of, or care about the concerns of, their populations, but there are also several "backlash states." These are states with particularly problematic national and international agendas, and they are often associated with refugee movements.

SOVEREIGN NATION-STATES: THE RAMIFICATIONS TODAY

The term "state sovereignty" is an important concept to understand because it influences how governments or international organizations do or do not respond to refugee movements. For much of the world, the concept of state sovereignty relates to the fact that some group within a society has power over territory and over people within the borders of that state. Sovereignty in such a situation is largely an issue of power.

In the United States, an administration assumes power through an election; we have a constitution, there are checks and balances, procedures, and laws. But it is not like that everywhere. There are many cases where a struggle for power can be as simple as some men with guns taking control of a capital city. If they can hold power over people and territory for (sometimes) just a little while, they can begin to achieve the recognition of other sympathetic states. Over time, they gain recognition, and that recognition and acceptance entitles them to membership in the international organizations that shape how we respond to refugees and many other aspects of life.

In fact, a state can become a member of the U.N., and most other international organizations, even if its government does not particularly care about what it does on behalf of the civilians for whom it has become responsible. The U.N. and many international organizations function like the trade associations of governments and thus are biased in favor of governments. This bias toward protecting the rights and the prerogatives of sovereign states is embedded in the charters of the U.N. and most international organizations.

People's prerogatives, people's rights, people's desire for development, freedom, peace, and justice—while often represented in international organizations—are not embedded in the charters and constitutions of these organizations to quite the same extent as are the prerogatives and rights of sovereign states. They are set forth mostly as aspirations of the human race. One eloquent statement of such aspirations is the Universal Declaration of Human Rights. There are many others, but they do not have the force of law in the way the prerogatives of states do. Indeed, many international politicians deal quite cynically with human rights, maintaining a supportive public posture but taking a very different position in the "smoke-filled" rooms where the decisions actually get made. However, the international community is getting better at dealing more forcefully with the aspirations and the rights of people. There are mechanisms for promoting those rights and aspirations.

REFUGEES: THE HISTORICAL CONTEXT

Refugees are a unique phenomenon within the broader context of migration. One could trace the existence of refugees as far back as the children of Israel, but the current approach to refugees has largely been developed since World War II. Between 1945 and 1951, there were many refugees in the world (during that time, they were called "DPs," displaced people). These DPs were "left over" from World War II, and there were not established mechanisms in many cases for resolving their situation. The Cold War was upon us. The Iron Curtain had descended, and the world was polarized into two opposing camps. The newly formed U.N. tried to improve its mechanisms for dealing with refugees. In 1951, a Convention Relating to the Status of Refugees was adopted, producing our current basic legal framework and structure for dealing with refugees.

The U.N. defined refugees as persons who are outside the borders of their home country, and who are fearful of returning because they fear persecution at the hands of their government because of their race, religion, political opinions, nationality, and/or membership in a particular social group. It created the United Nations High Commissioner for Refugees (UNHCR), one of the specialized agencies of the U.N. system. UNHCR is an agency that makes a positive difference in the lives of refugees, and it can do so in part because the United States government gives it very significant financial and logistical support.

When people flee their government and cross a border, they are in a place where they have no regular legal standing. The UNHCR was created to protect the rights of refugees in the same way that foreign embassies protect the rights of their nationals in another country. When refugees cross a border, the last place they can go to for help is the embassy of their government, so they turn to the UNHCR "High Commissioner." Most of us are not familiar with the term, but a High Commissioner is what the British call their ambassadors. The High Commissioner is an ambassador, a designated authority whose role it is to protect and assist an individual. The core of the system is the idea that UNHCR will protect the individual, assist them, meet their needs, and seek solutions to their predicament. That solution can be resettlement, and it can also mean, perhaps after a period in asylum, going home—what is called "voluntary repatriation."

INTERNALLY DISPLACED PEOPLE

"Internally displaced people" represent another group who are, legally, in worse shape than refugees. An internally displaced person is essentially a refugee who never crossed the border of his or her home country. The internally displaced are uprooted because they have been persecuted by their government but were either unable or unwilling to cross an international border. Throughout the last four decades, the international community has left internally displaced people to be largely the concern of their own sovereign government—the very government persecuting and attacking them in the first place. There are 22 million or more internally displaced people in the world today, a number that is growing and largely beyond the reach of the regular mechanisms of the international community.

AFTER THE COLD WAR

In the late 1970s and 1980s, as the Cold War was reaching its crescendo, the world experienced a number of severe regional conflicts. These regional conflicts were local wars that had some kind of connection to the larger confrontation between East and West. These conflicts consumed much of the world and its resources for over four decades in countries such as Vietnam, Afghanistan, Cambodia, Ethiopia, Angola, Mozambique, El Salvador, Nicaragua, Guatemala.

They were often called "low-intensity wars," a significant misnomer for the people caught in their crossfire. Low-intensity wars were brutal struggles in which huge numbers of people were killed and uprooted. Physical infrastructures, economies, and health systems were destroyed.

In just two examples of which most Americans were unaware, Angola and Mozambique, UNICEF said that the daily fatal impact of these wars on children was the equivalent of a Boeing 747 full of children crashing, with no survivors, every 24 hours. If you extrapolate these numbers to include the rest of the population, you can imagine the massive loss of life that occurred day after day. UNICEF used another paradigm in talking about the changes taking place in the way we wage war today. It said that during World War I, 90 percent of casualties were military, 10 percent were civilian. In World War II, more than 50 percent of the casualties were civilian. In today's low-intensity wars, more than 90 percent of the casualties are civilian.

During the Cold War, the West's reasons for caring about refugees were both humanitarian and political. It was almost always the case that they were fleeing from "the other side" and they were trying to get to "our side." It was almost always the case that the causation of the war was related to what we could identify, perhaps even legitimately, as the "enemy." We could understand that our motivations for helping these terribly unfortunate victims were not only an outpouring of our humanitarian concern—our motivations were not just good in and of themselves—but were also good for us. Our concern was an extension of our politics.

The Cold War is over; to those of us in the refugee field, this is exceedingly clear. For us, the demise of the Cold War means that the entire "bipolar" world—and with it much of the rationale for why people responded constructively to refugees—has been swept away. In place of the Cold War, we have a degree of chaos that has taken the concept of a "New World Order" and stood it on its head.

Rampant nationalism has replaced the bipolar discipline that the Cold War provided in many regions of the world. We now see power struggles of the most brutal kind. We see drives for self-determination that are often in themselves admirable. But within the context of the artificiality and lack of legitimacy of many states, there is an extraordinary pattern of state instability. States that are not viable in many senses of the word are producing truly large numbers of refugees, but today this often stimulates only localized concerns, as opposed to the globally overarching concerns of the Cold War conflict.

In many conflicts today, civilians are targeted intentionally. In the post-Cold War world, that alone is not necessarily enough to produce a productive response. That was what happened in Bosnia and Rwanda, in the cultural cleansing of an isolated group called the Nuba people in the Nuba Mountains of the central Sudan, and in a number of other places.

Increasingly, these dynamics are leading to what are called "complex humanitarian emergencies," which are often internal to a state and therefore beyond the normal reach of the international community's old mechanisms for assisting civilian victims. These human-itarian emergencies are often part of a civil war, and involve massive displacement, weak state structures, and tentative initiatives by the international community because we have not worked out all the mechanisms for dealing with these situations in the post-Cold War context.

Today, there are more than 15 million recognized refugees in the world. There are also three to five million people in what are called "refugee-like" situations, people who do not quite fit neatly into the refugee definition, but who look like real refugees. The number of refugees has been fairly stable for the last few years due, in part, to some good news: people do go home. In the last five years, about eight million Cold War refugees have gone home, but they are being replaced by the kind of refugees being produced by this new generation of wars and struggles.

"Our" interests are not as clear anymore. Why in the world should the people of the former "Free World" care if "those people" want to kill each other off? We might have cared before because we were afraid of the Soviets, but why should we care now? Isn't it time, now that we have won the Cold War, to turn to the needs of our own society? The answer is, yes. But in my judgment, it is never the case that we should pit one set of victims against another. We ought to be focusing on both sets and recognizing that they are both getting the short end of the stick.

The U.N., when it set up UNHCR, thought that it would take three years to resolve the world's refugee problem! Yet, 45 years later there is a blizzard of information that comes to us each day, and it is easy to be overwhelmed by it. Some people would say that the humanitarian rationale for still caring is very weak, that you need a realpolitik reason. People say we should be focusing on improving our competitiveness and meeting our own needs. I do not denigrate that point of view. I just think we can do more than one thing at one time.

Refugees Today

The United States and Europe are no longer looking at refugees as a humanitarian issue. Instead, refugees are on our security agenda. The talk is about crime, terrorism, drugs, and refugees. These days we talk about "prevention"—a term that has been distorted beyond all recognition. Prevention of what? Prevention of the causes that uproot people? Or are we trying to prevent the refugees themselves from somehow impinging on our lives? We set up "safe haven zones." But if you were in Srebrenica, you knew that not only was it not a safe haven zone, it was one of the least safe places in all of Bosnia.

Listen to the terminology used by politicians when they are discussing this topic. They tend to promote the idea that all refugees are simply just seeking jobs. They tend to suggest that refugee motivations do not justify our responding to them as real people but, rather, as numbers and as a threat. They suggest that we need to be suspicious of why refugees are fleeing. The newest prevention principle influencing international debate about refugees today is about denying them access, reducing the number that come to the United States, for example, from Haiti, by interdicting them and sending them back. In the case of Cuba, even though we officially denounce that government, we send refugees directly back. This principle of denying access holds not only for the United States but for many of the countries of the world today—not only the developed but, increasingly, the less developed as well. Many nations do not take the plight of refugees seriously. They do not take their politics seriously. And they do not seem to take even their deaths seriously. Evidence of this can be seen on television daily.

Inaction: The Case of Rwanda

Rwanda is a country that I have been involved with for the last 15 years. Perhaps a million Rwandans were killed in about ten weeks during the months of April, May, and June, 1994. The United States, and most of the other governments of the world, presented it as a "mindless tribal slaughter." They suggested that civilians were being killed in a civil war.

That was not the case. It was one of those struggles in a reasonably artificial state in which people whose power was threatened wanted to keep that power and privilege so much that they were prepared to exterminate an entire portion of that country's population to do so. The extermination was national in scope. It was institutionalized and coordinated: the heads of the state security forces and all civil authorities participated in perpetrating this crime against humanity. It was political, and it was genocide. Most of the world did not even know at the time that it was happening. The extermination largely succeeded. Probably 90 percent of the targeted population were killed, changing the demographics of that country forever. Until now, there has been no punishment for the perpetrators. When they left Rwanda, they took the national treasury with them, and some of them are living very well in France, Kenya, and other countries. I know a family in California who has spent the last year and a half tracing their extended family in Rwanda. They can count more than 600 who were killed and only two who are surviving. The international community was not present. The government of Rwanda was sitting on the U.N. Security Council at the time of the genocide—the very government that perpetrated this crime. The words of Edmund

Burke are still undeniably true: "The only thing evil needs to triumph is for good people to do nothing."

HOW CAN WE REACT?

I traveled throughout Rwanda with the soldiers of the army that ended the genocide. I went into villages as they established control, into the churches (many people were killed in churches) at the same time they did. I saw what they saw. The experience brought me back to the fact that the life of every individual human being is infinitely valuable, and the kind of freedom and opportunities we have in this country are so precious they must never be taken for granted.

It also brought me back to the fact that I, as one individual, am accountable for responding to things like this. Increasingly, this has become my philosophy of life, and it has renewed my drive to rescue people—in this case, people who would have been refugees if they had survived. My belief is that it was never right for us to think that responding to refugees was somehow good for us. The only enduring rationale in my view is their intrinsic value as people, not their value to us.

First of all, I suggest that it is terribly important for the U.S. to refocus its approach to foreign policy (and domestic policy as well) around the principle that people ought to be our genuine priority. They should be central to our foreign policy and to the way we respond, in particular, to refugees. I believe that one can make other, pragmatic realpolitik arguments. But a humane focus ought to be at the core of our policy. We need a popular constituency to help produce this, because you cannot leave it to politicians, in this or any other country, to take that course of action. I believe that common people tend to have higher morals than do the politicians and the governments that represent them.

I hope that institutions, through their local mechanisms, engage in community education about the role of the medical and nursing professions in responding to refugees. The American Academy of Nursing, for instance, might consider establishing a foreign affairs working group. The Academy could meet with those who represent refugee organizations in the United States and elsewhere to see what advocacy, education, and services can be developed together. It is not as hard as one might think. All of the nongovernmental agencies that work in the refugee field belong to a single organization in Washington, D.C. called InterAction.

Secondly, we need to reorient the U.N. The rights and aspirations of people are less strongly protected by the U.N. than are the rights of its sovereign member states, no matter how barbarous they are to their own people. This situation needs to be rectified. There should be standards for member states. When a government significantly abuses its civilian population, there ought to be clear and meaningful steps taken against it. We need to define the international community's responsibilities when governments "go bad." And we need to apply the U.N. laws we have.

The one international crime that we do have a law against is genocide. We have the Genocide Convention which says what states are obliged to do when genocide occurs. Senator William Proxmire went to the U.S. Senate almost every day for about 30 years and pleaded for U.S. ratification of the Genocide Convention, and, finally, the United States ratified it. But when genocide has occurred, our government has not always invoked this treaty. We have to make sure that when the U.N. and other international organizations talk about prevention, it is prevention of the causes that made civilians refugees in the first place, and not the prevention of refugees from "bothering" us.

Third, it is important to figure out what the international community's obligations are with respect to internally displaced people. Having a system for dealing with refugees who cross a border is admirable, but if people can't escape that does not mean we should abandon them to their fate. There should be a way of responding more adequately to the protection and assistance needs of internally displaced people.

Fourth, in this country and others, we need to understand and defend the right to asylum. The vast majority of people who seek asylum do so legitimately—they did not leave their homelands on a "joy ride." They need to flee, and they need to find some receptivity. They need to find asylum. The principle of asylum is under attack today, and it is important to be aware of this fact.

And, lastly, it is terribly important to uphold our own ethnic and racial diversity in the United States and make it work. It is important to take real steps to cross existing racial and ethnic boundaries within our local communities. It is also important to understand and respond accordingly to individuals in one's own community or when refugee situations are covered in the media. These are all individuals, and no one has the right to write-off their identity. This needs to be the basis, in my view, of our morality.

There will continue to be large, perhaps growing, numbers of refugees, internally displaced people, and others who merit the kind of response and attention that I have described in this paper. I hope the health care community will share my resolve to provide a humane, humanitarian response to them.

Protection and Health Needs of Refugee Women and Girl Children

JUDITH A. MAYOTTE, PH.D.
Special Adviser for Refugee Issues
Bureau of Population, Refugees, and Migration
United States Department of State

The post-Cold War global transitions confronting us today, and their implications for health care, are complex and profound. In the wake of such transitions, millions are affected by war and civil conflict. My experience has been with those who have been uprooted by conflict, especially the women and children who make up 75 percent to 80 percent of the world's approximately 50 million refugee and internally displaced civilians. All have been through the trauma of flight and loss with grave effects on their health and well-being.

In this paper, I will discuss some of the most critical health issues affecting refugee women and girl children in refugee and internally displaced camps. I will focus particularly on the protection refugee women and girl children need against acts of sexual violence and on the related area of their comprehensive reproductive health needs.

Overview

Our television screens bring us face-to-face with the incalculable human suffering caused by conflicts raging in many parts of the world. In 1991, following the Persian Gulf War, we were numbed at the sight of a sixty-mile stretch of humanity as two million Iraqi Kurds fled Saddam Hussein's forces, inching through mud and relentless rain into the rugged northern mountain terrain that separates Iraq from Turkey and Iran.

Even that massive movement of people did not prepare us for what we saw in Rwanda in the spring of 1994. Following the massacre of at least 500,000 Tutsis and moderate Hutus, the world witnessed an exodus of a magnitude never before seen in such a short space of time and to such an uninhabitable area as people fled from Rwanda to Tanzania and to the Goma region of Zaire. A quarter of a million fled into Tanzania in the space of 48 hours at the end of April 1994; this number was small in comparison to the one million who crossed into Zaire within a four-day period in mid-July 1994. Goma is a rocky and desolate volcanic place, and it was almost impossible to gain access to adequate, potable water or to dig latrines to ensure necessary sanitation facilities. People bathed, washed clothes, defecated, and drew drinking water from Lake Kivu, a lake in which dead bodies floated.

The death, chaos, and feelings of helplessness were more than many relief workers could bear. A sea of people on the move, with many dropping beside the road to die, was all there was to be seen. Digging graves in the volcanic land was difficult, and people were dying so fast that bodies lay in piles, decomposing. The Zairian government even enlisted Zairian Boy Scouts to assist in burying bodies. It was a human disaster and a public health nightmare.

In this upheaval, as in others around the world, women, children, and the elderly made up the greatest bulk of the population and suffered more. Diarrheal diseases—mainly cholera and dysentery—took many lives. Early on, clinics established by the well-equipped relief organization *Medecins sans Frontieres* (MSF) began to assist those who had the strength to get to the clinics.

Barbara Smith, a seasoned relief worker and a clinical psychologist, is Vice President of Overseas Programs for the International Rescue Committee (IRC), the largest U.S. nonsectarian refugee relief organization. In her visit to the camps in the Goma area, she immediately ascertained inequities in refugee access to goods and services. It was the strongest who pushed forward for food and water and the strongest who received clinical care. Her mission was to find a way to bring lifesaving assistance to the weaker members of this massive refugee population. She walked through Kibumba camp, one of the most populous, several times and discovered one particularly isolated area where the refugees appeared to be the most needy.

Dr. Smith described her difficulties in getting to these people. First of all, she had to find a chief who was willing to assist her, deal with the chaos in the area, and protect the medicines and oral rehydration solution she and her team brought to the area. The chief was responsible for making a list of the very sick who needed to be seen in their huts. The first list of 500 were all men. It was only when the medical team went inside the tents and huts that they discovered many severely ill women and girl children. Dr. Smith's mission was accomplished despite these obstacles, and within a week six IRC medical teams were operating in three areas of the camp, focusing on primary health care that was community-based. IRC sanitarians began constructing latrine platforms and installing them over holes the refugees dug.

That the chief listed only male refugees when Dr. Smith sought out the very sick in Kibumba camp was not unusual. Among many refugee populations, women are either ignored or seen as more expendable than men. They have their own particular needs, however. Refugee and internally displaced women, having gathered up their children and fled their villages, towns, and cities, often face not only the loss of a spouse but the daunting prospect of being the head of a household. If these women are to survive and nurture children, and if they are to live and not simply exist in their radically altered circumstances, their special needs must be addressed, particularly their need for protection against sexual violence.

Protection Needs Against Sexual Violence

"We have lost the picture of ourselves." In the city of Mostar, in Bosnia, a young Muslim woman, one of a group of women who had been sexually assaulted, spoke these halting words to a delegation from the Women's Commission for Refugee Women and Children. To lose the picture of yourself is to lose your spirit—your soul—your self. These women wanted to reclaim what was theirs in the depth of their being.

A 15-year-old's story tells it best. I will call her Emina. Although her small town in eastern Bosnia-Herzegovina was predominantly Muslim in population, Croats, Serbs, and Muslims lived there together, peaceably. Emina loved going to school and dreamed of becoming an engineer or an architect. Then everything changed.

"It happened so fast," Emina recalled. "One day we lived together peacefully, and the next our Serbian neighbors were dragging us from our homes. Many of us women were violated in front of our families and neighbors before we were taken to the school house and imprisoned. Many of our fathers and brothers were killed or taken away." Emina, her mother, and her sisters were taken to the gymnasium and crowded among some 250 other women. Others were jammed into classrooms. Over and over they were abused and raped until one day, several months later, they were freed in an exchange of prisoners.

When I was alone with Emina, she began to draw on a plain white sheet of paper. She showed me her drawing, an architectural rendering of the school building. At the far right end was the huge gymnasium. A hallway connected it to the rest of the school and all the classrooms where she had learned mathematics, languages, history, science, and art. In the same building where her dream to be an architect or an engineer emerged, it was shattered. In that sketch, however, as professional as any architect's drawing, I could see the dream was still alive. Emina was struggling to recapture the picture of herself.

Emina and the other women were persecuted because of who they are ethnically. As civilians, the attacks on them and their subsequent imprisonment were calculated. Rape was used as a weapon of war. It was part of the Bosnian Serb military strategy to terrorize Bosnian Muslim civilians and cause them to flee their homes. These women were no longer byproducts of war; they were targets. In the Bosnian and Rwandan conflicts, sexual violence was used as a weapon to the point where rape became one of the tactics of war.

Addressing the protection needs of refugee women is critical, particularly protection against sexual violence, exploitation, and discrimination as well as protection in terms of assuring access to food and assistance. In flight and at borders of entry into a country of asylum, women frequently are targets of sexual abuse. Attacks may be random acts of violence, or they may involve a demand for sexual favors in return for proper documentation or access to relief goods.

I remember a young Cambodian woman who, while fleeing her country after the defeat of Pol Pot, fell into the hands of unprincipled Cambodian soldiers. They held her at their base in the forest for months. During the day, they raped her and forced her to work for them. At night, when they went off to fight, they tied her to a tree so she could not escape. When she became pregnant and no longer of use to them, the soldiers let her go. Relief workers who received and cared for her knew there was little likelihood that she would every fully recover spiritually or physically. She was one among the tens of thousands of women who fall prey to soldiers during flight.

Even when women reach a camp, they are not safe. Often, military personnel from the host country—examples are Thai soldiers among the Cambodians and Zairian soldiers with Rwandans—rape and abuse women with impunity at night when the expatriate relief workers are no longer present. Life in crowded refugee and internally displaced settings provokes brutality, not only from strangers but from family members. One relief worker described such a camp as "a time bomb on a short fuse." Domestic violence rises as the months extend into years and many despair of ever returning to their homelands.

Protection and Access to Assistance

Protection and access to assistance are integrally interwoven. For widows and women whose husbands are fighting, the cost of receiving food rations frequently entails giving sexual favors to male refugees who are given the rations to distribute. Other women are forced into prostitution to obtain adequate food for themselves and their children. Even without payment in sexual favors, food distribution is typically highly inequitable. Women heads of households often receive fewer food rations. As a consequence, they and their children have higher rates of malnutrition than do families headed by males. If women were placed in charge of food distribution, not only would there be greater equity and safety in distribution, but less would be sold or siphoned off for military use.

Often the layout of a camp is dangerous for women. Latrines may not be in sight of living quarters, and camps are rarely well lighted. The source of water may be a distant and secluded river or stream; so, too, the place for gathering wood. Simple precautions such as night patrols and improved lighting in camps can make a world of difference for many unaccompanied refugee women. The preventive presence of qualified people along escape routes, in camps, during refugee-status determination procedures, or wherever women are most at risk will save many of them from sexual abuse. Camp dangers can be resolved only if women are involved in the design and determination of camp location, in decision making, and in the creation, development, and implementation of programs.

Refugees themselves must be given support and the means to improve the protection of refugee women and girl children. Ensuring realistic opportunities for education and skills training of refugee women, thereby enabling them to provide for themselves and their dependents, will make them far less vulnerable to sexual abuse. Many situations would improve with an increase in the numbers of female protection officers and personnel in camps. Even though males are primarily the perpetrators of sexual assaults, the majority of protectors for female refugees are males. Most refugee women fear taking their stories to anyone, especially male officers or counselors, and so remain silent. As a result, the perpetrator often is not apprehended, charged, or convicted and is, in fact, allowed to strike time after time.

Reproductive Health Needs

Another key area of consideration is the comprehensive reproductive health needs of refugee and internally displaced women and girl children. Attention to these needs is critical to the survival of refugee populations because reproductive health is critical to general health. What do I mean by comprehensive reproductive health? The Cairo Platform for Action from the 1994 United Nations International Conference on Population and Development defines it as follows:

"Reproductive health is a state of complete physical, mental, and social well-being and not merely the absence of disease or infirmity, in all matters relating to the reproductive system and to its functions and processes. Reproductive health therefore implies that people are able to have a satisfying and safe sex life and that they have the capability to reproduce and the freedom to decide if, when, and how often to do so."

The platform emphasizes that reproductive rights embrace certain human rights already recognized in various international human rights instruments and in other documents reflecting international consensus. These rights apply equally and without discrimination to refugees, for, as the Cairo Platform notes:

"Migrants and displaced persons in many parts of the world have limited access to reproductive health care and may face specific serious threats to their reproductive health and rights. Services must be sensitive particularly to the needs of individual women and adolescents and responsive to their often powerless situation, with particular attention to those who are victims of sexual violence."

Reproductive health care must include: pre- and post-natal care for pregnant women and maternal/child health care for mother and infant, as well as education about and care of HIV infection and AIDS, other sexually transmitted diseases (STDs), and numerous gynecological conditions; family planning; prevention of sexual violence and exploitation of women and counseling for women who have been assaulted; and protection against unsafe abortions.

Recipients of comprehensive reproductive health care should be not only pregnant women but, also, adolescent girls, single or non-child bearing women, and elderly women. Emphasis should be placed on preventive health practices rather than simply curative care. Among refugee populations, care providers should look beyond the emergency phase of a humanitarian crisis to development and education in the maintenance phase as well as to a future beyond exile for these women.

To the end that the comprehensive reproductive health needs of refugee women and girl children be met, the Women's Commission for Refugee Women and Children, the only organization dedicated specifically to advocating for refugee women and children, embarked on a groundbreaking field study among refugee women to determine how these needs could be addressed. Following the publication of the 1994 study, *Refugee Women and Reproductive Health Care:* Reassessing Priorities, the Reproductive Health for Refugees Consortium was created to focus on five essential and complementary areas of reproductive health: maternal care, family planning, HIV/AIDS/STDs, sexual and gender violence, and safe abortion-related issues and services.

The U.S. Government is a leading advocate for the development and implementation of policies to protect and assist refugee women, and it works closely with the United Nations

High Commissioner for Refugees (UNHCR) to develop and issue written policies and guidelines covering protection of and assistance to refugee women. The challenge now facing UNHCR and the international community is the implementation of these policies and guidelines in operations in
the field.

Assistant Secretary of State Phyllis Oakley, who heads up the Bureau of Population, Refugees, and Migration (PRM), gives the reproductive health needs of refugee women and girl children a top priority in her efforts on behalf of refugees. She recognizes the connections between women's development and reproductive health and between refugee protection and reproductive health. Assistant Secretary Oakley now asks nongovernmental organizations (NGOs) requesting funding for public health programs from PRM to include a broader reproductive health component in their proposals. In addition, she strongly urges senior personnel of the refugee organizations through which PRM channels funding to include a strong and comprehensive program emphasis on reproductive health in the context of overall refugee protection and assistance.

Under the strong leadership of Sadako Ogata, UNHCR is also addressing the critical needs of women refugees. Its *1991 Guidelines on the Protection of Refugee Women*, its *1995 Guidelines on Prevention and Response to Sexual Violence against Women*, and its *1995 Field Manual on Reproductive Health in Refugee Situations* are important documents that need to be read and implemented operationally within the UNHCR and by NGOs, both at headquarters and in the field. Progress in implementation is being made thanks to the monitoring efforts of the Women's Commission, PRM, and other organizations.

The overall reproductive health needs of refugee women and girl children also include maternal care, family planning, and HIV/AIDS/STD education, prevention, and treatment. Over the years in refugee settings, maternal and child health programs have benefitted innumerable refugee women during pregnancy and delivery, both are points at which complications are a leading cause of death. Enhanced training of traditional midwives (sessions that I have had the joy of sitting in on) has saved the lives of millions of mothers and infants. Outreach into the refugee community by women community health workers and traditional birth attendants identifies women with high-risk pregnancies and provides home-based care and safe deliveries, thereby lowering refugee maternal and infant mortality rates.

While refugees who have crossed a border and survived the initial emergency phase in a crisis benefit from maternal and child health programs, many of the internally displaced civilians (approximately 25 million to 30 million) are not so fortunate. While we are all conscious that rape has been used a weapon of war in the Bosnian War and other conflicts, we are not so aware that the withholding of food and medical supplies from civilian displaced people has also been used as a brutal weapon of war.

The conflict in southern Sudan is a case in point. During one of my trips there, the government of Sudan was prohibiting NGOs from distributing relief to internally displaced civilians in rebel-held territory. Close to 125,000 southern Sudanese civilians had fled a government offensive and gathered in the strategically important border area near Nimule.

There I met with a group of midwives who told me that because they did not have access to relief supplies, they did not even have clean razor blades with which to cut the umbilical cords in the birthing process. They could not provide immunization against tetanus or supply supplementary iron to combat anemia. Care providers were helpless in the face of rampant diarrheal disease because they lacked a remedy as simple as therapeutic oral rehydration solution.

We know how the lack of food contributes to untimely deaths in adults and children. Without proper nutrition, pregnant women face a double jeopardy of miscarriage, or, as a result of anemia, fatal hemorrhaging during childbirth. Not only must they be assured of access to adequate food—food that is fortified with vitamins and minerals—but, also, access to safe drinking water and basic health and other relief assistance. Too many are denied such access.

Family planning and counseling services should become an integral part of refugee health services. Populations who have lost people to genocide—such as the Cambodians, southern Sudanese, Rwandans, and Bosnian Muslims—want to repopulate as quickly as possible fearing that if they do not, their cultures may die. But too many pregnancies in too short a time jeopardizes these populations in the long run because of the toll it takes on the women who are the child bearers and nurturers. The already fragile health of the majority of refugee women, exacerbated by inadequate food intake and a lack of proper sanitation facilities, becomes even more precarious when pregnancies are not spaced with enough time for women to recover from the previous one. Both mother and newborn suffer. Little attention has been given to the need for birth spacing and birth limitation.

During the emergency phase of a humanitarian refugee-producing crisis, family planning is not high on anyone's agenda because energies are channeled into saving lives and providing basic, critical needs for survival such as food, shelter, safe water, and basic medical assistance. Often in emergencies, after the trauma of flight, many women do not have regular menstrual cycles. Consequently, conception rates are frequently low. But regaining health and realizing the implications of the deaths of large segments of their populations, many women feel (or are pressured to feel) it is their duty to help their country repopulate quickly. Most women refugees do not come from cultures in which family planning through various means of birth control is widespread. Although the cultural, moral, and religious norms of a given refugee population must be given critical consideration, the post-emergency phase can be an opportune time to educate refugees in responsible family planning and for offering choices for birth spacing and birth limitation.

It is imperative to devise effective and appropriate care for and education about HIV infection, AIDS, and other STDs among refugee populations along with comprehensive strategies to prevent and combat them. We know that "HIV spreads most quickly in conditions of poverty, powerlessness, and social instability" (UNHCR 1995 *Field Manual on Reproductive Health Needs in Refugee Situations*). I can think of no populations more vulnerable to HIV infection, AIDS, and other STDs than refugee and internally displaced populations, particularly refugee women and girl children who are victims of sexual violence more frequently during war and conflict than in times of peace. In the developing world and among refugee populations, AIDS and HIV infection is transmitted primarily through heterosexual intercourse. Education must reach out to men as well as to women, and all must take responsibility for preventing and combating these diseases.

Summary

With all their losses, I have found the vast majority of refugee and internally displaced women to be women of uncommon resilience. They remain the backbone of their communities and are the nurturers of the future generation being born in exile. Just as they are the ones who must reestablish the family in exile, they are also the ones who recreate the familial environment upon returning to their homelands. It is, therefore, critical to attend to their health and welfare if their cultures and nations are to survive and thrive.

International Humanitarian Law and the Nursing Profession:
The Current Framework and Challenges Ahead*

MICHAEL HOFFMAN, J.D.
Officer, International Humanitarian Law
American Red Cross

All opinions expressed in this paper are those of the author and are not necessarily the opinions of the American Red Cross.

INTERNATIONAL HUMANITARIAN LAW

More than at any time in the past half century, nursing professionals today are asked to take action in circumstances of armed conflict.[1] Armed conflicts generate an extraordinary need for the full spectrum of health services, ranging from immediate emergency medical care to the long-term rehabilitation of public health infrastructure. For nursing professionals to operate effectively in these difficult environments, with the largest possible margin of safety, they must understand the basic rules of *international humanitarian law* (IHL). IHL is the body of rules and principles utilized in saving lives and alleviating suffering during armed conflict.

It is a well-established expectation that modern health care professionals should play an exclusively humanitarian role in times of war and peace alike. It is also significant that this was not always the established expectation. One centuries-old precedent foreshadows some fundamental questions facing the modern nursing profession, albeit appearing today in more subtle form.

The role of medieval military nursing orders deserves some attention when considering the challenges facing nurses in the 1990s. These orders were renowned for excellent patient care, but they also had martial branches devoted principally to the waging of war. Nursing *and* combat were their business.[2] In our time, medical workers are usually accorded special protection during armed conflict, but to maintain that status they may not mix the duties of nurse and knight.

The Geneva Conventions

While it is obvious that the armored knight-nurse mix would be troublesome under the terms of modern IHL, there are some modern role-mixing dilemmas that merit careful consideration from nurses and other health care professionals. These will be elaborated on later.

The IHL protections accorded medical personnel during armed conflict are set forth in the Geneva Conventions of 1949. To maintain their special status, medical personnel must abstain from assuming any roles as combatants and devote themselves entirely to their medical duties. The full protection of the Geneva Conventions of 1949 applies during conflict between or among two or more nations—circumstances referred to as international armed conflict. These conventions form the critical component of IHL used to protect medical personnel and facilities in zones of armed conflict.

Nurses and other medical personnel are protected persons under the Geneva Conventions of 1949, meaning that they are not to be attacked or held as prisoners of war, and they must at all times be respected while carrying out medical services for the wounded and sick of armed forces and civilians.[3] Medical units and transport under military control are not to be attacked, and these personnel signal their protected status by wearing an armlet bearing a red cross on a white field.[4]

Civilian hospitals organized to care for the wounded, sick, and others in need of medical care are also protected by the Geneva Conventions. The rights and duties of medical personnel were expanded in the two Protocols to the Geneva Conventions of 1949 that were adopted by a diplomatic conference in 1977. The protocols further develop IHL relating to medical personnel during international and internal armed conflicts, but the core rules and protection of IHL are still contained in the 1949 conventions. The Geneva Conventions have been ratified by the United States and almost every other country in the world. To date, the United States has not ratified the protocols.

Geneva Conventions: Limitations on Protection

Protected status is not offered open-ended, however, for everyone performing medical services in a zone of armed conflict. Individuals and organizations joining in spontaneous efforts to rescue and care for the wounded and shipwrecked in the aftermath of battle are protected by the Geneva Conventions, but extended protection is only available to those personnel expressly authorized to perform these services under the conventions. Medical and support personnel assigned to military medical duties, and like personnel serving full-time in civilian hospitals, possess such authority. They are entitled to wear the protective armlet and are entitled to the protection set forth for medical workers in the Geneva Conventions.

Civilian nurses and other civilian medical personnel serving in zones of armed conflict, but without official authorization under the terms of the Geneva Conventions as described, do not possess the protected status of medical personnel. They are entitled to protection as civilians under the Geneva Convention Relative to the Protection of Civilian Persons in Time of War. However, they cannot expect that parties to a conflict will acknowledge a right to carry out medical duties under special status.

Internal Armed Conflict

Armed conflict within one nation—referred to as internal armed conflict—is the kind that most nurses are likely to encounter in their international work. During such conflict, medical professionals' IHL-based privilege of humanitarian service and its accompanying protection are reduced in scope. IHL's more limited scope of application during internal armed conflict results from opposition, by governments, to internationally mandated humanitarian constraints on their response to an armed, organized domestic challenge. In internal armed conflict situations, most of the requirements of the Geneva Conventions do not apply. The Geneva Conventions only apply in their entirety during international armed conflict.

Common Article 3

Article 3, an article identical in each of the four conventions, does, however, set out the minimum standards that apply in internal armed conflicts. Among the other requirements of common Article 3 is that all parties to an internal armed conflict must assure that, "The wounded and sick shall be collected and cared for," and that, "An impartial humanitarian body, such as the International Committee of the Red Cross, may offer its services to the Parties to the conflict."

The International Red Cross and Red Crescent Movement

The International Committee of the Red Cross (ICRC) holds a unique, long-established customary right of initiative in situations that may require the services of a neutral and independent humanitarian intermediary. Pursuant to that right and the specific responsibilities set forth for the ICRC in the Geneva Conventions, the ICRC visits prisoners of war and civilian internees, provides medical services and delivers relief supplies in conflict zones, and furnishes tracing and family message services in areas of conflict when normal channels of communication have broken down. Under the right of initiative, the ICRC also visits political and security detainees and furnishes other services outside the context of international armed conflict.

The International Federation of Red Cross and Red Crescent Societies (the Federation) and National Red Cross Societies also render humanitarian assistance to victims of armed conflict under authority of the Geneva Conventions. Other organizations are not identified by name in the Geneva Conventions, but the treaties do provide terms under which they can furnish impartial humanitarian assistance during armed conflict.

The International Red Cross and Red Crescent Movement (the Movement)—composed of the ICRC, Federation, and National Societies—has a special role in protecting the integrity of IHL and nurturing its development. The Movement has played a leadership role in this field since the adoption of the earliest Geneva convention in 1864. Since 1867, that role has been highlighted at periodic International Conferences of the Red Cross, where the Movement meets with governments to assess the current state of IHL and determine what new measures may be needed to strengthen these rules.

INTERNATIONAL HUMAN RIGHTS LAW

The body of international law protecting human life and dignity in peacetime is known as *international human rights law*. While IHL provides a conceptual and operational framework for nursing professionals and other medical personnel during armed conflict, there is no comprehensive legal schema setting out their rights and duties during peacetime human rights and humanitarian challenges. In 1975, the International Council of Nurses (ICN) adopted a resolution setting forth guidance on the "Role of the Nurse in the Care of Detainees and Prisoners." In 1983, it adopted a "Statement on the Nurse's Role in Safeguarding Human Rights."[6] These resolutions serve as a source of guidance for nursing professionals though they do not constitute a source of international law. However, should these standards continue to be applied, they might eventually serve as the foundation for customary international law—a non-treaty-based form of international legal authority.

WHICH LAWS APPLY?

The 1990s have witnessed chronic, low-intensity violence going beyond peacetime disturbances (e.g., riots) but not rising to the level of internal armed conflict. At times it can be unclear whether to apply traditional rules of IHL or to apply international human rights law, leaving a legal gap that the nursing profession may have to cope with in the future.

In some recent armed conflicts there has been the added challenge of introducing IHL among peoples who have been isolated from the world for some generations or have otherwise received little or no exposure to this body of law. Finally, there are substantial challenges connected with armed humanitarian intervention under United Nations (U.N.) auspices. International law has not, to date, developed to accommodate an active but neutral military role on the battlefield. Because the U.N. is not a nation-state and cannot ratify the Geneva Conventions of 1949, some argue that U.N.-sanctioned military forces are not bound by those rules. Further, since such U.N. interventions are authorized for purposes that are stated to be impartial and humanitarian, it is sometimes argued that U.N.-sanctioned forces are not parties to a conflict but rather a neutral presence on the battlefield.

Because such units are authorized to deploy for humanitarian purposes, civilian relief and medical staff who rely on these units for protection may tend to assume that their impartial humanitarian role as care providers is complementary to the self-perceived neutrality of a U.N. military expedition. This is a potentially dangerous assumption and needs to be reconsidered by the nursing profession and other medical professionals.

Health care services during armed conflict are part of a growing, dynamic mosaic of humanitarian and human rights endeavors. They take place in environments not always easily classified within established IHL and human rights law. For nurses to understand their rights and duties in those settings (or lack thereof), they need to know the basics of IHL. Long-term policy planning may require a deeper understanding of both IHL and human rights law. The medieval warrior-nurse may seem an incongruous figure today. Nurses could, however, easily engage in activities that others may find equally incongruous —and perhaps equally threatening.

ISSUES FOR NURSES' CONSIDERATION

Policies and operating procedures may depend on time, place, and mission. Nurses engaged in human rights investigations, for example, may need to adopt an operational focus quite different from that of nurses delivering care on the battlefield. However, the conduct of nurses working in one of those settings might affect the safety and effectiveness of colleagues working in the other. The following issues are offered for consideration as the leadership of the nursing profession looks to the challenges ahead.

Issue One: *Is an advocate's role compatible with the humanitarian mission of nursing professionals in the field?*

The 1975 ICN resolution provided that nurses " having knowledge of physical or mental ill-treatment of detainees and prisoners take appropriate action including reporting the matter to appropriate national and/or international bodies."[7] Such action is important—sometimes indispensable—to the work of human rights advocacy groups. Medical personnel protected by the Geneva Conventions are expected to deliver humanitarian service impartially, and may in some cases be working under the control of an armed force hostile to the national or political interests of those workers. Is the reporting role compatible with the mission of nursing professionals when they operate in an armed conflict zone?

Issue Two: *Should a code of conduct be adopted to guide the activities of nursing professionals during armed conflict?*

As armed conflict environments become increasingly hazardous for all persons providing humanitarian service, and the legal lines that traditionally separated categories of conflict begin to erode, would a standardized code of conduct be useful in guiding activities and decision making in the field? Such a guide might assist in focusing on the work and needs of the nursing profession and avoid the pitfalls involved in following the policies and self-perceived roles of other actors in situations of armed conflict.

Issue Three: *Should training in international humanitarian law and human rights law be incorporated into education programming for nursing professionals?*

As international humanitarian issues gain increasing importance for U.S. health care professionals, is there a need for a curriculum that covers these issues? If so, would a single, standardized curriculum serve all needs, or would specialized programs be needed for nursing professionals who will need to engage in quick problem solving in the field or furnish long-term leadership for policy formulation?

Conclusion

The nursing profession plays a time-tested, historic role in alleviating the suffering among victims of armed conflict. IHL offers a time-tested road map for these efforts. IHL must also, however, remain adaptable to the new challenges of our time. The American Academy of Nursing is uniquely suited to facilitate debate on contemporary IHL issues that have an impact on the nursing profession and provide leadership in devising strategies to meet the challenges ahead.[1]

[1] *Armed conflict*, the term used in the Geneva Conventions, is used in this paper to denote a situation of organized, armed hostility between/among states or between/among factions within a nation. Armed conflict describes an actual state of facts. The term, *war*, is used only where one nation has formally declared itself to be in a state of armed hostilities against another nation. Because the term, armed conflict, is broader and includes more of the conflict environments where nurses will usually work, it is the term used.

[2] Stuart, I.M., and Austin, A. L. 1962. *A History of Nursing: From Ancient to Modern Times A World View,* 5th ed., pp. 52-57. New York: G. P. Putnam's Sons.

[3] For a detailed discussion of issues relating to the protection and identification of medical workers and medical facilities that are highlighted in this paper, see Baccino-Astrada, A. 1982. *Manual on the Rights and Duties of Medical Personnel in Armed Conflicts. Geneva: International Committee of the Red Cross and League of Red Cross and Red Crescent Societies.*

[4] The Red Crescent is also an authorized protective emblem under the Geneva Conventions and serves that protective role in some nations. Although not in the Geneva Conventions, the Red Shield of David, used in Israel, is also a respected emblem.

[5] Haroff, Tavel, M. 1993. Action taken by the International Committee of the Red Cross in situations of internal violence. *International Review of the Red Cross* 294 (May-June): 205.

[6] Stover, E., and Nightingale, E., eds. 1985. *The Breaking of Bodies and Minds*, pp. 276-279. New York:W. H. Freeman and Company.

[7] *Ibid*, p. 277.

A Global Profile of the Immigrant/Migrant Child

MARY LOU DE LEON SIANTZ, PH.D., R.N., F.A.A.N.
Associate Professor, Psychiatric-Mental Health Nursing
Indiana University School of Nursing

Background

A surge in immigration to the United States during the last 20 years has been followed by the explosive growth of ethnically diverse immigrant families and children. The increasing diversity has enormous implications for the health, social welfare, and educational institutions that prepare the nation's children for participation in a pluralistic world.

The recent influx of immigrants who also have relatively high rates of birth is an especially important factor for those concerned with the health and welfare of children and the social policies that affect their well-being. While the number of people migrating to the United States is comparatively small in a global context, it is similar to the level that occurred at the turn of the century (Grantmakers Concerned with Immigrants and Refugees [GCIR] 1994).

Many factors precipitate migration, chief among them the changing patterns of economic development that create opportunities for individuals to move. Other causes include poverty, natural disasters, and political instability. The current national debate on immigration has ignored the needs of children and their families. Similar to other periods of immigration, concerns about its effects have focused largely on the labor force and public expenditures. Attention to immigrant children and their families, and the barriers they face in becoming healthy and contributing members of our society, is needed. However, knowledge, research, and intervention strategies concerning this group are lacking.

Children remain "invisible" until they have been described, counted, and publicly addressed. This is particularly true of disenfranchised groups like immigrant children. Policies and programs that support immigrant children and their families must build on knowledge that identifies how best to serve them. To counterbalance concerns about the costs of immigration, knowledge is also needed to enlighten the public about the contributions of immigrants. Policy, programs, and interventions that assure the health and well-being of immigrant children must build on longitudinal information about the range of developmental trajectories that these children experience and the factors that promote or keep them from attaining their potential in society.

While much is already known about the effects of poverty, racism, and trauma on children, research on immigrant children, especially the young immigrant child—knowledge about second language acquisition, ethnic identity formation, etc.—is almost nonexistent. This knowledge is crucial for understanding the health and development of the immigrant child.

Along with the growth in the immigrant child population in many urban and rural school districts, there have also been increases in academic, health, and behavior problems (Carlin 1990; Gibbs and Huang 1989). Yet, pediatric, school, and child/adolescent psychiatric nurses and other child health care professionals have been unprepared to handle such problems. With the current explosion in the child immigrant population, the need for developing nursing research, curricula that prepare nurses, interventions, and social policy that specifically address this culturally diverse sector has never been greater (Siantz 1993).

This session: a) discussed global trends and factors that have an impact on immigrant and migrant children's physical and mental health; b) introduced a framework that helps conceptualize and examine what is known and unknown about this broad and complex topic; c) identified implications for nursing research, education, and practice; and, d) made policy recommendations that support the health and welfare of children experiencing global transitions.

MIGRATION: GLOBAL TRENDS AND CHARACTERISTICS

Global Migrants

Estimates are that 100 million people are on the move today globally (Meissner et al. 1993). Migration occurs in three patterns, with the majority migrating within their own countries. The next largest group represents people migrating from a less-developed country to a more-developed country with which it shares a border. A relatively small group of migrants are living in countries that share borders with developed countries and who migrate to them (Meissner et al. 1993). The United Nations High Commissioner for Refugees (UNHCR), the U.N. agency that is responsible for refugee assistance and protection, has estimated that in 1993 there were about 18 million refugees worldwide. In 1980, there were less than 8 million. An additional 24 million have been involuntarily displaced within their own countries in refugee-like situations. They are unable to cross international borders (GCIR 1994).

The majority of refugees can be found in Africa (5.7 million) and the Middle East (5.6 million). An additional 3.2 million live in Europe, primarily Eastern Europe, 2.3 million in South and Central Asia, and 400,000 in East Asia and the Pacific. There are 140,000 in North America and 108,000 in Latin America and the Caribbean (U.S. Committee for Refugees 1993).

When citizens are displaced, it is largely a result of a breakdown in their home government, an external aggressor abusing the country's citizens, or the home government's inability to function (U.S. Committee for Refugees 1993). Because the decision to migrate can be influenced by a combination of economic, social, and political factors, migration should be considered in the context of environmental, developmental, foreign policy, political, and human rights issues.

FACTORS HAVING AN IMPACT ON GLOBAL MIGRATION TRENDS

Political Factors

During the last 10 years, an overwhelming and unforeseen global trend toward the democratization of political systems has occurred, accompanied by a much greater participation of people in determining their own future. In spite of the end of the cold war, however, tensions between East and West and regional and local conflicts and warfare have developed or continued. The benefits of peace are only slowly emerging. Few, if any, resources have thus been available for human development (World Health Organization [WHO] 1995). At the same time, refugees and displaced persons have increased in numbers, and so have their multiple health care needs.

Economic Factors

In other areas of the world such as the Americas, for example, attempts to integrate and share problem-solving approaches have resulted in economic integration pacts and agreements to liberalize trade among nations—e.g., the North American Free Trade Agreement (NAFTA) and the Southern Common Market (MERCOSUR). Another sign of peaceful coexistence has been the emergence of collaborative political initiatives such as the Latin American Parliament (PARLATINO) (WHO 1995). In 1994, this trend toward cooperation culminated in the Summit of the Americas in Miami. During this meeting, leaders from 34 countries worked toward integrating their economies, liberalizing trade, strengthening their democratic institutions, and improving their general development (WHO 1995).

Despite these trends, privatization and decreasing investment in social sectors such as education and health have resulted in increasing inequities in health care delivery, particularly in mental health (Pan American Health Organization [PAHO] 1994). Socioeconomic and political changes have, in part, contributed to the mental health problems prevalent in the Americas. These problems include violence; weakening of the family structure; anxiety and depression; effects from political repression and human rights violations; social fragmentation and weakening of social support; psychosocial suffering among children, youth, and the elderly; substance abuse; chronic mental illness; and unhealthy working and living conditions (PAHO 1995).

Long-term growth and the ability of the world economy to supply goods and services has led to improvements in material standards of living for some of the world's population (WHO 1995). Poverty has continued, however, and will remain a major world problem. Poverty is the single major determinant of individual, family, and community health. The number of poor people has increased substantially both in the developing world and among the underprivileged groups and communities within developing countries, especially in the slums of big cities. During the second half of the 1980s, the number of people in the world living in poverty increased and was estimated at over 1.1 billion in 1990. This is more than one-fifth of humanity (WHO 1995).

FACTORS INFLUENCING IMMIGRATION TO THE UNITED STATES

Historical Factors

Immigrant communities in the United States today have been related to this country's history of international military, political, economic, and cultural involvement and intervention, particularly in the Asian and Latin American and Caribbean Basin regions.

In the post-World War II period, legal immigration to the Untied States has been associated with family preferences in the allocation of immigrant visas and by kinship networks developed over time, rather than by economic cycles and deliberate recruitment (Jasso and Rosenweig 1990). This particular family trend has had tremendous implications for children. These are addressed later in this paper.

At the beginning of the century, 67 percent of all immigrants were men. As of 1941, the majority (55 percent) of immigrants have been women (U.S. Immigration and Naturalization Service [INS] 1994). Since 1970, most immigrants legally admitted to permanent residency have come from Asia and Latin America and the Caribbean. The 19.8 million foreign-born persons counted in the 1990 Census were the largest immigrant population in the world in absolute terms. In relative terms, only 7.9 percent of the population of the United States was foreign-born, a lower proportion than at the turn of the century (INS 1994).

Displacement, Labor, and Family Reunification

In the United States, the immigrant of today reflects a polarity that ranges from the very poor, uneducated manual laborer, to the well-off, highly educated professional. This polarity exists in very different historical and structural contexts than in the past. For example, among political refugees and asylees, admission to the United States began with the 1948 Displaced Persons Act. This was the first legal act to officially recognize refugees in the United States (Rumbaut 1995b).

The number of undocumented laborers began to increase after the termination of the Bracero Program in 1964. This program was initiated to meet the labor shortages in the southwest during World War II but continued during the postwar years of rapid U.S. economic expansion. This group has continued to increase since the passage of a 1965 law which abolished the national-origins quota system and gave greater priority to family reunification over occupational skills. Until this law was passed, Western Hemisphere immigration had not been restricted (Rumbaut 1995b). With the passage of the 1990 Immigration Act, the immediate relatives of adult citizens can enter without limit.

Changes in the U.S. immigration laws, which abolished the national origin quota system and changed the preference system to give greater priority to family reunification over occupational skills, have been the principal reason for the new immigration and the change in the national origins of its composition. For children, the family helps to define their experiences in the United States, with the family structure and dynamics key to their success (Board on Children and Families 1995).

Proposed Immigration Reform

Although the United States is admitting more immigrants than ever before as a result of a liberal immigration policy, there is little official thought given to ways of integrating new immigrants into American society. It is this mismatch that has precipitated various contentious proposals before Congress (Fix and Zimmerman 1995). For example, spending on bilingual education increased 4 percent, while the number of limited English proficient children increased 65 percent during 1995. Aid to state and local governments which provides $50 per child to help with their integration is targeted for elimination. Few targeted federal dollars exist to assist schools in integrating these children.

A reduction in the numbers of immigrants and their economic impact on the United States are the overall goals of proposed legislation. Restrictions on which family members can enter, who can bring in family, and a redirection of immigrants ready to enter are being carefully developed with a shift in responsibility from the government to the family. A family sponsor must demonstrate an income that is 200 percent above the poverty line. Adult siblings and adult children will not be allowed to join their families. For an adult parent over 65 years of age, proof of health insurance must be provided before he or she will be allowed to immigrate. Inherent in these laws is the reduction of family supports so important to immigrant families. This reduction will have many negative implications for parents and children (Fix and Passel 1994).

Countries of Origin

Immigrants to the United States have come from over 140 different countries, with some regions and countries over-represented in spite of the equitable numerical quotas provided to each country by United States law since 1965. Immigration from the more developed countries has declined over time while that from the developing countries has increased. The more developed countries include Canada and most European countries. About half of all Europeans and Canadians came before 1960. Many British, German, and other European scientists and professionals came to the United States after World War II to pursue opportunities not available to them in their own countries. By 1960, the postwar economy in their own countries had so improved that the need to immigrate decreased. Japanese immigration, which accounted for the majority of Asian immigrants after World War II, has also declined, remaining stable and small over time with half consisting of marriages to U.S. citizens (Rumbaut 1995b).

According to the INS, from 1960 to 1993 Mexico has been by far the largest source of legal immigration to the United States, accounting for over four million admissions, with the Philippines ranking second at over one million. These two countries have strong linkages with the United States that date back to the Mexican and Spanish-American Wars during the last century, as well as long histories of dependency relationships, external intervention and colonization, and decades of active agricultural labor recruitment. These trends preceded the establishment of family networks and group migrations. The extensive United States military presence in the Philippines has also increased immigration through marriages with U.S. citizens stationed there. Sociologists have found that the presence of an American military base in the country of origin has been one of the most powerful factors determining the number of immigrants admitted as wives of U.S. citizens (Jasso and Rosenweig 1990).

American post-world-war foreign policy provides insight into other sizable migrations from different world regions. For example, Vietnamese, Cambodians, and Laotians have immigrated as political refugees as a result of the Vietnam War. Soviet Jews and Poles have immigrated as refugees since the end of the Cold War in 1989 and the collapse of the Soviet Union in 1991. From Latin America, Salvadorans, Guatemalans, and Nicaraguans have fled civil wars and worsening economic conditions. Cubans entered during the 1960s as a result of Castro's takeover. Thousands of Chinese students after Tiananmen Square and Iranians after the 1979 revolution have also been issued immigrant visas.

Mexico is by far the main source of both documented and undocumented immigration. Mexico accounted for over one-fourth of the 22.6 million immigrants estimated from the 1994 Current Population Survey and over two-thirds of the nearly 3 million formerly undocumented immigrants who have been legally admitted under the amnesty (Rumbaut 1995b).

Occupational Characteristics

Huge differences exist in the occupational backgrounds of immigrants. Highly skilled immigrants have migrated from India, South Korea, the Philippines, and China since the 1960s. Their proportions have increased since the passage of the 1990 Immigration Act which increased employment-based visas. Highly educated Japanese, Canadians, and British have also immigrated. In contrast, legal immigration from Mexico, El Salvador, the Dominican Republic, and, until recently, Italy, has consisted largely of manual laborers and low-wage service workers. This is also the case for refugees from Laos, Cambodia, Vietnam, Cuba, and Haiti.

Concentrations in the United States

Most immigrant children and their families are concentrated in six states: New York, Florida, Texas, Illinois, New Jersey, and California. Seventy-eight percent of all recent immigrant students attend school in California, Florida, Illinois, New York, and Texas, with 45 percent in California alone (U.S. Department of Education 1991). The total schoolage population in the United States is projected to grow by more than 20 percent over the next twenty years, from 34 million in 1990 to 42 million in 2010. It is estimated that immigrant children will account for more than half of this growth. Immigrant children will increase to 9 million in 2010, representing 22 percent of the schoolage population (Fix and Passel 1994).

Children: A Global Perspective

Every year, more than 145 million children are born in the world. The short existence of many is marked by pain, disease, and early death. During the last decade, more than 1.5 million children were killed in wars, and more than 4 million were physically disabled. More than 5 million were forced into refugee camps, and more than 12 million lost their homes (UNICEF 1993). Ten million suffered mental health problems (Organizacion Panamericana de la Salud [OPS] 1995).

In spite of all the setbacks that have occurred globally, according to UNICEF (1993), more progress has been made in the last 50 years than in the previous 2,000. Since the end of World War II, the average incomes of the developing world have more than doubled. Infant and child death rates have been more than halved. The proportion of the developing world's children starting school has risen to more than three-quarters. Polio has been eradicated (PAHO 1995). Within a decade, child malnutrition, preventable disease, and widespread illiteracy could be overcome (UNICEF 1993). Global political and economic changes in the world are starting to create conditions which offer renewed hope for overcoming the worst aspects of world poverty, especially as they affect the world's children.

Health and Mental Health Status

Health status worsens over time for many immigrant children and families. Research has documented that on every measure of health status, immigrants who have lived in the United States for five years or less were healthier than foreign-born persons who had lived here 10 or more years (Stephen et al. 1994). Among Mexican-American mothers, those who are recent immigrants are more likely to give birth to healthy fullterm infants, experience fewer physical problems during pregnancy, and breast feed for longer periods than their American-born Mexican female counterparts (Siantz 1996). Interestingly, for many immigrants health practices exist within the culture that protect mothers. These include insuring appropriate food intake, rest, and support from the family network during pregnancy, labor, and delivery. These diminish over time in the United States.

United States-born Mexican-Americans who experience poverty are more likely over time to develop the diseases of poverty—alcoholism, drug abuse, depression—than are those who were born in Mexico. In a recent study that aggregated data across all immigrant groups, it was found that on every measure of health status, immigrants who had lived in the United States five years or less were healthier than foreign-born persons who had resided in the United States for at least ten or more years (Stephen et al. 1994).

These findings may be due to immigrants arriving with existing physical conditions that are masked during their initial settlement period. They may develop high-risk health behaviors over time such as drinking, smoking, or other changes in their lifestyle. On the other hand, because health status is so highly correlated with family income, if it declines over time, poor health may be due to socioeconomic factors (Carlin 1990; Stephen et al. 1994).

These families are also less likely to have access to a regular source of health care because their work does not provide health insurance, or they cannot afford it. As children grow and develop, they seek health care for acute problems but not for prevention or early intervention. If a mother has not sought prenatal care, it is unlikely that she will seek well-child care as her child grows and develops.

Immigrant children and families in the United States face conflicting social and cultural demands while trying to acculturate to a new host country whose welcome can range from inviting to discriminatory, even hostile. Both children and parents must deal with loss, separation, and family disruption in addition to stress from the migration itself. Children and their families must adapt to a new and very different social, cultural, linguistic, and climactic environment (Laosa 1989). It is easy to understand why both parents and children are at risk for depression from the stress of migration (Esquivel 1990; Golding and Burnam 1990).

Migration and acculturation require children to deal with stress, particularly from loss of familiar surroundings and significant persons in the child's life (Garcia-Coll 1995). The reaction to loss is affected by their stage of development. During early childhood, emotional support is sought from parents rather than friends who are playmates. Consequently, they may more easily leave their friends than they might otherwise later in life (Maccoby 1983). A young child is more likely to obey his or her parents' decision to migrate while an adolescent may challenge his or her parents' decision. Separation from primary caretakers will be more stressful for children 6 months to 4 years than for an older child. It is during this period that children establish selective attachments and begin to maintain relationships during a period of separation (Garcia-Coll 1995). Cognitive development will also affect the grief reactions of children (Rutter 1983).

While migrants encounter stress, refugees frequently encounter additional stress because of the nature of their pre-departure experiences (Rumbaut 1991). Among Central American refugees, exposure to war was the strongest predictor of stress (Leslie 1993). Refugee children have been overlooked because they cannot speak for themselves, and they are overshadowed by the needs that adult refugees express (Eisenbruch 1988).

Refugee children, in particular, experience violence, loss, and severe deprivation which place them at risk for posttraumatic stress disorder (PTSD) (Athey and Ahern 1991; Rumbaut 1991). The symptoms and severity of the reaction are associated with the degree of violence, presence or absence of personal injury, age of the child, and access to family support (Athey and Ahearn 1991; Munroe-Blum et al. 1989). Children who remain with their biological family have lesser signs of psychological disturbance because of the stronger bonds that develop from the crisis the entire family shared (Ressler, Boothby, and Steinbock 1988).

Acculturation

The process of acculturation requires that an immigrant child integrate the culture of his or her parents into the mainstream culture in which he or she lives. It has been reported that immigrant parents expect their children to become bicultural and bilingual. They are expected to not only maintain their cultural heritage and native language but also adopt strategies that will make them successful and accepted by their host country (Lambert and Taylor 1990). One of the major difficulties in accepting two cultures is the transgenerational-transcultural conflicts it causes. As children are encourage to succeed, they become alienated from the culture of their homeland. The normal generational conflict that parents and children experience is exacerbated when socialization occurs in different cultures leading to parent-child conflicts (Cropley 1983).

Biculturalism

While immigrant children in the past were considered to be torn between two worlds, a more recent concept of biculturalism has emphasized the ability of persons to function effectively in two or more cultures without negative effects (Ogbu 1994). What this means is that children can live in two cultures by becoming competent in the cultural beliefs and values of both cultures (LaFramboise, Coleman, and Gerton 1993).

Ethnic Identity

Migration has an impact on a child's social and ethnic identity development, particularly during adolescence as he or she develops in a context that might be racially and culturally different from the host culture (Garcia-Coll 1995). Historically, ethnic identity has often been defined as ethnic labeling. More recently, it has been suggested that it has several dimensions: self-categorization, knowledge, attitudes, and feelings, as well as behaviors related to one's culture (Bernal et al. 1990; Rosenthal and Hrynevich 1985). Ethnic minority children learn about their ethnicity and ethnic group memberships through social learning experiences provided by families and communities, as well as the dominant society. As they develop, particularly cognitively, they learn more complex information and integrate past learning with present learning (Bernal et al. 1990).

Language in particular has been linked with the formation and maintenance of an ethnic identity. Those who speak English are more likely to identify themselves as American. On the other hand, those who are fluent in their national language are more likely to select that national identity. Those who are bilingual are more likely to select hyphenated identities (e.g., Mexican-American, Chinese-American) (Rumbaut 1995ba).

Impact of Parenting

Immigrant children are part of a family and cannot be considered in isolation. Family structure and dynamics and parental mental health and behavior have a direct impact on a child's well-being (Board on Children and Families 1995). There is a long history of research on the negative impact of difficult life circumstances on family life. For example, stressful conditions such as poverty, large families, crowded living conditions, and unemployment are related to hostile and rejecting maternal behaviors, maternal depression, and a poor prognosis for a child's development (McLoyd and Wilson 1991).

Conversely, parenting behavior that is sensitive to a child's personality, capabilities, and to the developmental tasks he or she faces encourages a variety of highly valued developmental outcomes which include social competence, intellectual achievement, and emotional security (Baldwin and Cole 1982; Belsky 1984; Rutter 1990). During the preschool years, high levels of parental nurturing and control encourage the ability to engage peers and adults in a friendly and cooperative manner (Baumrind 1971; Belsky 1984; Garmezy 1990; Luthar and Ziglar 1991). This trend continues through the school years with parental use of induction or reasoning, consistent discipline, and expressions of warmth (McCall, Applebaum, and Hagarty 1973; Garmezy 1990).

An example of research on the Mexican-American migrant farmworker child and family has underlined the importance of parental social support for a child's peer acceptance and school behavior (Siantz 1994). Migrant fathers and mothers had different sources of social support within and outside the family. Fathers in particular sought support outside the home. Mothers and teachers had differing views of the child's behavior, which may be due to differences in behavior that the child exhibited at home and at school. Feeling overlooked at home, the child may misbehave to seek maternal attention. On the other hand, he or she may behave in school out of respect for the teacher and to comply with rules. Such behavior is expected by traditional Mexican families of their children when outside the home.

The research findings further suggested the importance of identifying mothers and fathers who are isolated or lack access to spouse, partner, family, and friends. This lack of access, along with the consequent isolation, could have deleterious effects on their children's behavior at home and achievement at school (Siantz 1994).

Risk and Resilience

Why do some immigrants successfully adapt to their new environment, in spite of unusually challenging circumstances, and excel beyond the academic and social norms of U.S. natives, while other do not adapt positively? Among Hispanics, the prevalence of educational and mental health problems rises as a function of length of time in the United States (Baral 1979; Borjas and Tienda 1985; Canino, Earley, and Rogler 1980; Valdez 1986). Evidence suggests that Hispanics vary widely in their coping strategies, adjustment, development, and adaptation (Laosa 1990; London 1990). Their vulnerability to the events and processes associated with their immigration and settlement experiences also varies. Among Vietnamese, Laotian, Hmong, Cambodian, and Filipino immigrant children, Rumbaut (1995) has found that while time in the United States is strongly predictive of improved English reading skills, longer residence in the United States as well as birth in the United States is associated with declining academic achievement and aspirations. Students whose parents are both immigrants outperform their counterparts whose mother or father is native-born. Increased parent-child conflict strongly predicts lower grade point averages

(GPAs), lower aspirations, and lower math scores. However, having a peer group composed of co-ethnic friends who are also children of immigrants has a positive effect on GPAs. The positive influence of such friends who may also be oriented toward achievement may extend to math and reading scores as well as higher aspirations.

Figure 1 presents an analytic model of the joint influences hypothesized to predict child outcomes. It is a model applied in my research with Mexican-American migrant farmworker children and their families. It is not meant to be all-inclusive, but, rather, to provide a framework for the consideration of the joint influences that have an impact on child outcomes. Represented within this figure are the key concepts of resilience theory—risk and protective factors and child outcomes. Much of what has been presented can fit under these categories.

Figure 1. Theoretical Model of Resilience

Relationship of Risk and Protective Factors to Child Outcomes

Risk Factors	Protective Factors	Child Outcomes
Family stress	Parent characteristics	Maladapt/Adapt
Poverty	Child characteristics	Academic Failure/ Academic Success
Migration		Behavior Problems/ Mental Health
Loss/Separation		Isolation/Bicultural

The model builds on Garmezy's (1985) and Laosa's (1990) framework on stress and resilience and has been extended to include concepts relevant to successful outcomes among immigrant and migrant children. In this model, differences in environmental, family stress (risk factors), and parent and child characteristics (protective factors) are expected to influence child outcomes (adaptation or maladjustment). It emphasizes the joint importance of both parent and child characteristics on child outcomes. For an immigrant child, positive outcomes resulting from migration need to be highlighted. For example, research has identified the positive academic benefits that result from speaking two languages. This is a result mainly of a larger part of the brain being used in the process.

The concept of risk implies the identification of biological, psychological, social, and environmental factors that increase the probability of negative outcomes for children (Garmezy and Masten 1990). Protective factors are presumed to inhibit the expression of negative child outcomes. They are those attributes of persons, environment, and events that appear to ameliorate predictions of poor adaptation based upon an individual's risk status (Rutter 1990). Factors that have been found to protect children include: a) child characteristics of problem-solving ability, even temperament, and perceived social competence, as well as health status; b) family cohesion; and c) the availability and use of external support systems by both parents and children.

More and more research has identified the importance of focusing on competence and positive child outcomes instead of on maladjustment in the presence of risk. In addition, immigrant children need to be studied in their own right disregarding the view that a "control" group is needed for adequate interpretation.

Conclusion

Not since the days of the public health nursing movements in New York City at the turn of the century has the role of nurses been so necessary for the implementation of innovative health and mental health practices, policies, and research that meet the needs of the new immigrant population.

What is unique about this modern-day challenge is that it is global as well as national. This challenge considers context as well as history, the individual as well as the family, the very young as well as the elderly. American nurses will increasingly need to collaborate and join forces with our international nursing colleagues to develop policies and practices that are of global as well as national benefit to the world's immigrants. The challenges that the global migration and immigration of children and families has given nurses is the need to develop a comprehensive approach that encompasses nursing education, nursing practice, nursing research, and health policy. The following discussion briefly highlights issues that should be considered in these areas.

Recommendations

Education

In preparing pediatric, child/adolescent psychiatric, school, and community health nurses to work with children, educators should:

- require a foreign language.

- integrate research methodologies specific to minority and immigrant populations into research courses for both undergraduate and graduate students.

- require cross-cultural clinical experiences of all nursing students.

- integrate knowledge about the impact of migration, immigration, and acculturation on parenting and the growth and development of children.

- provide a historical perspective on U.S. immigration trends.

Practice

In providing nursing interventions with immigrant children and their families, nurses should understand what benefits they will receive from:

- identifying interventions that maximize benefits for children and families while respecting their cultures, histories, beliefs, and migration experiences.

- supporting immigrant parents and their children and identifying parents who are isolated or lack access to social supports.

- providing in-service education for nurses to develop cultural competence with immigrant children and their families.

- empowering immigrant children to care for themselves.

- encouraging interdisciplinary collaboration.

- developing community partnerships that build on trust and adaptation to a new society through a healthier beginning.

Research

Research involving immigrant children should include:

- the testing of new models.

- a focus on positive outcomes.

- longitudinal studies that track the developmental and health trajectories of immigrant children.

- studies of sub-populations that consider within-group variance and contextual factors.

- the development of research partnerships with immigrant groups.

- awareness of the challenges and economics of conducting research with an immigrant sample.

- sensitivity to the fact that many immigrant parents are suspicious of researchers' motives.

- investment of financial and human resources to bridge the chasms created by the cultural and class differences that exist between researchers and immigrant participants.

- awareness that recruitment into and retention of immigrant children and parents in research projects can be stressors for those families and participation may be a low priority.

Policy

Nurses need to consider public policy development and its implications for children and their families from both a national *and* global perspective. Public policy must make recommendations that support the integrity of the family and all of its members as well as their health and welfare. It should also acknowledge the potential contributions that immigrants can make to their host countries. Public policy should support ways to integrate immigrant families into their host countries' societies. Such policy considers the well-being of immigrant families, assures the developmental potential of children from a life span perspective, and respects their cultures, histories, beliefs, and migration experiences.

References

Athey, J.L., and Ahearn, F.L. 1991. The mental health of refugee children: An overview. *In Refugee children:* Theory, research, and services, J. L. Athey and

F. L. Ahearn, eds., pp. 1-19. Baltimore: The Johns Hopkins University Press.

Baldwin, A.L., Cole, R.E., and Baldwin, C.P. 1990. Parental pathology, family interaction, and the competence of the child in school. *Monographs of the Society for Research in Child Development* 47 (197).

Baral, D.P. 1979. Academic achievement of recent immigrants from Mexico. *Journal of the National Association of Bilingual Education* 3(13): 1-13.

Baumrind, D. 1971. Current patterns of parental authority. *Developmental Psychology Monographs* 4(1): 1971.

Belsky, D. 1984. The determinants of parenting: A process model. *Child Development* 55: 83-96.

Bernal, M.E., Knight, G.P., Garza, C.A., Ocampo, K.A., and Cota, M.K. 1990. The development of ethnic identity in Mexican-American children. *Hispanic Journal of Behavioral Sciences* 12: 3-24.

Board on Children and Families Commission on Behavioral and Social Sciences and Education, National Research Council, Institute of Medicine. 1995. Immigrant children and their families: Issues for research and policy. *The Future of Children* 5(2): 72-89. Los Altos, CA: The Center for the Future of Children, The David and Lucile Packard Foundation.

Borjas, G.J., and Tienda, M., eds. 1985. *Hispanics in the U.S. economy*. New York: Academic.

Borneman, eds., pp. 223-224. Austin, Texas: Hogg Foundation for Mental Health, the University of Texas.

Canino, I.A., Earley, B.F., and Rogler, L.H. 1980. *The Puerto Rican child in New York City: Stress and mental health.* New York: Hispanic Research Center, Fordham University.

Carlin, J. 1990. Refugee and immigrant populations at special risk: Women, children and the elderly. In *The mental health of immigrants and refugees*, W.H. Holtzman and T.H.

Chud, B. 1982. The threshold model: A conceptual framework for understanding and assisting children of immigrants. In *Uprooting and surviving*, R. C. Nann, ed., pp. 95-99. Boston: D. Reidel Publishing Company.

Cropley, A.J. 1983. *The education of immigrant children*. London: Croom Helm.

Eisenbruch, M. 1988. The mental health of refugee children and their cultural development. *International Migration Review* 22(2): 282-300.

Esquivel, G., and Keitel, M. 1990. Counseling immigrant children in the schools. *Elementary School Guidance and Counseling* 24: 213-220.

Fix, M., and Passel, J.S. 1994. *Immigration and immigrants: Setting the record straight.* Washington, DC: The Urban Institute.

Fix, M., and Zimmerman, W. 1995. *Immigrant families' well-being and public policy: A deepening divide*. National Symposium on International Migration and Family Change: The Experience of U.S. Immigrants (November 2-3, 1995). Pennsylvania State University.

Garcia-Coll, C. 1995. *The effect of migration on child development*. National Symposium on International Migration and Family Change: The Experience of U.S. Immigrants (November 2-3, 1995). Pennsylvania State University.

Garmezy, N. 1985. Stress resilient children: The search for protective factors. In *Recent research in developmental psychopathology*, J.E., Stevenson, ed. Oxford: Pergamon Press.

Garmezy, N., and Masten, A. 1990. Assessing, preventing, and reaching childhood. In *Childhood*, L. E. Arnold, ed., pp. 459-474. New York: McGraw-Hill.

Garmezy, N., and Tellegen, A. 1984. Studies of stress resistant children: Methods, variables, and preliminary findings. In *Applied developmental psychology*, F. J. Morrison, C. Lord, and D. P. Keating, eds., vol. 1, pp. 231-287. New York: Academic.

Gibbs, J.T., and Huang, L.N. 1989. A conceptual framework for assessing and treating minority youth. In *Children of color*, J. T. Gibbs and L. N. Huang, eds., pp. 1-29. San Francisco: Jossey-Bass Publishers.

Golding, J., and Burnam, M.A. 1990. Immigration, stress, and depressive symptoms in a Mexican-American community. *The Journal of Nervous and Mental Disease* 178(3): 161-171.

Grantmakers Concerned with Immigrants and Refugees (GCIR). 1994. *Newcomers in America: A grantmaker's look at immigrant and refugee issues*. New York: The Joyce Mertz-Gilmore Foundation.

Immigration and Naturalization Service (INS), U.S. Department of Justice. 1994. 1993 *statistical yearbook*. Washington, DC: U.S. Government Printing Office.

Jasso, G., and Rosenzweig, M. 1986. Family reunification and the immigration multiplier: U.S. immigration law, origin-country conditions, and the reproduction of immigrants. *Demography* 23: 291-311."". 1990. *The new chosen people: Immigrants in the United States*. New York: Russell Sage Foundation.

LaFramboise, T., Coleman, H.L., and Gerton, J. 1993. Psychological impact of biculturalism: Evidence and theory. *Psychological Bulletin* 114: 395-412.

Lambert, W.E., and Taylor, D.M. 1990. Language and culture in the lives of immigrants and refugees. In *The mental health of immigrants and refugees*, W.J. Holtzman and T.H. Bornmeman, eds., pp. 103-128. Austin, Texas: Hogg Foundation for Mental Health, the University of Texas.

Laosa, L. 1984. Social policies toward children of diverse ethnic, racial, and language groups in the United States. In *Child development research and social policy*, H.W. Stevenson and A.E. Siegel, eds., pp. 1-109. Chicago: The University of Chicago Press."'. 1990. Psychosocial stress, coping, and the development of Hispanic immigrant children. In *The mental health of ethnic minorities*, F.C. Serafica, A.I. Schwebel, R.K. Russell, P.D. Isaac, and L.B. Myers, eds., pp. 38-65. New York: Praeger Publishers.

Leslie, L. A. 1993. Families fleeing war: The case of Central Americans. *Marriage and Family Review* 19(1/2): 193-205.

London, C. 1990. Educating young new immigrants: How can the United States cope? *International Journal of Adolescence and Youth* 2:81-100.

Luthar, S., and Zigler, E. 1991. Vulnerability and competence: A review of research on resilience in childhood. *American Journal of Orthopsychiatry* 1(1):6-22.

Maccoby, E.E. 1983. Socio-emotional development and response to stressors. In *Stress, coping, and development in children*, N. Garmezy and M. Rutter, eds., pp. 217-234. New York: McGraw-Hill.

McCall, R.B., Appelbaum, M.I., and Hagarty, P.S. 1973. Developmental changes in mental performance. *Monographs of the Society for Research in Child Development* 38 (3 serial n. 150).

McLoyd, V., and Wilson, L. 1991. The strain of living poor: Parenting, social support, and child mental health. In *Children in poverty*, A. C. Huston, ed., pp. 105-135. Cambridge: Cambridge University Press.

Meissner, D., Hormats, R.D., Walker, A.G., and Ogata, S. 1993. *International migration challenges in a new era: A report to the Trilateral Commission*, p. 1. New York: The Joyce Mertz-Gilmore Foundation.

Munroe-Blum, H., Boyle, M.H., Offord, D.R., Kates, N. 1989. Immigrant children: Psychiatric disorder, school performance, and service utilization. *American Journal of Orthopsychiatry* 59(4): 510-519.

Ogbu, J. 1994. From cultural differences to differences in cultural frame of reference. In *Cross-cultural roots of minority child development*, P. M. Greenfield and R. R. Cocking, eds., pp. 365-392. Hillsdale NJ: Lawrence Erlbaum Associates Publishers.

Organizacion Panamericana de la Salud (OPS). 1995. *La salud de los ninos en las Americas: Un compromiso con nuestro futuro.* Comunicacion para la salud no. 7. Washington, DC: Oficina Sanitaria Panamericana, Oficina regional de la Organizacion Mondial de la Salud.

Pan American Health Organization (PAHO). 1994. *Health conditions in the Americas.* Washington, DC: Pan American Sanitary Bureau, Regional Office of the World Health Organization.

"'. 1995. *The development of community mental health nursing services in the southern cone: Argentina, Brazil, Chile, Paraguay, and Uruguay.* Washington, DC: Pan American Health Organization, Division of Health Service Systems, and Promotion and Protection of Health.

Ressler, E.M., Boothby, N., and Steinbock, D.J. 1988. *Unaccompanied children: Care and protection in wars, natural disasters, and refugee movements.* New York: Oxford University Press.

Rosenthal, D.A., and Hrynevich, C. 1985. Ethnicity and ethnic identity: A comparative study of Greek-Italian and Anglo-Australian adolescents. *International Journal of Psychology* 20: 723-742.

Rumbaut, R. 1991. The agony of exile: A study of Indochinese refugee adults and children. In *Refugee children: Theory, research, and services*, F. L. Ahearn and J.L. Athey, eds., pp. 53-91. Baltimore: The Johns Hopkins University Press.

"'. 1995a. The crucible within: Ethnic identity, self-esteem, and segmented assimilation among children of immigrants. *International Migration Review* 28:748-794.

"'. 1995b. *Ties that bind: Immigration and immigrant families in the United States.* National Symposium on International Migration and Family Change (November 2-3, 1995). Pennsylvania State University.

Rutter, M. 1983. Stress, coping, and development: Some issues and some questions. In *Stress, coping and development in children*, N. Garmezy and M. Rutter, eds., pp. 1-41. New York: McGraw-Hill.

"'. 1990. Psychosocial resilience and protective mechanisms. In *Risk and protective factors in the development of psychopathology*, J. Rolf, A. S. Masten, D. Cicchetti, K. H. Nuechterlein, and S. Weintraub, eds., pp. 181-214. Cambridge: Cambridge University Press.

Siantz, de Leon, M.L. 1993. Child and family minority research: How are we doing? *Journal of Child and Adolescent Psychiatric Nursing* 6(4): 6-9.

"'. 1994., Parental factors correlated with developmental outcome in the migrant Head Start child. *Early Childhood Research Quarterly* 9(3 & 4): 481-504.

"'. 1996. A profile of the Hispanic child. In *Health needs of Hispanics*, S. Torres, ed., pp. 13-35. New York: National League for Nursing Press.

Simons, J., Finlay, B., and Young, A. 1991. *The adolescent and young adult fact book.* Washington, DC: The Children's Defense Fund.

Stephen, E.H., Foote, K.K., Hendershot, G.E., and Schoenborn, C.A. 1994. Health of the foreign-born population: United States, 1989-90. *Advance data from vital and health statistics of the Centers for Disease Control and Prevention.* Hyattsville, MD: National Center for Health Statistics.

United Nations Children Fund (UNICEF). 1993. *The state of the world's children.* New York: Oxford University Press.

U.S. Committee for Refugees. 1993. *World refugee survey*, p. 51: Washington, DC: the Author.

U.S. Department of Education. 1991. *The condition of bilingual education in the nation: A report to the Congress and the president.* Washington, DC: the Author.

Valdez, R.B. 1986, Feb. *A framework for policy development for the Latino population.* Testimony prepared for the Second Annual California Hispanic Legislative Conference.

World Health Organization (WHO). 1995. *The world health report 1995: Bridging the gaps.* Geneva: Office of World Health Reporting, the World Health Organization.

Women across the Life Span:
A Working Group on Immigrant Women and Their Health

JULIENE G. LIPSON, PH.D., F.A.A.N.
Professor, University of California, San Francisco

BEVERLY McELMURRY, PH.D., F.A.A.N.
University of Illinois, Chicago

JUDITH LaROSA, PH.D., F.A.A.N.
Tulane University

As individuals and as members of the American Academy of Nursing (AAN), if we are to intervene for the health and well-being of immigrant women, we must develop appropriate initiatives for action. These initiatives can and must be implemented at many levels, from our own individual actions to those which affect our communities, regions, and, ultimately, the nation. To accomplish these tasks, we must unite to reach common goals because there is great strength in a thoughtful, integrated approach by such a powerful and respected organization.

INTRODUCTION

The 1995 American Academy of Nursing Annual Meeting and Conference, "Health Care in Times of Global Transitions," dealt in part with the implications of global transitions and cultural identity for health and illness of individuals, families, and communities. The session on women across the life span was timely in the context of the 1990's explosion in women's health research encouraged by governments at the state and national levels. The focus of the AAN conference went beyond the majority of national efforts to include areas that have received little attention, specifically, immigrant women's health.

A backdrop for the session on women across the life span was an olive paper, "Immigrant Women and Their Health: A Time to Take Heed" (Meleis, Lipson, and Muecke, in press) which focused on the issues facing women who immigrate to the United States, either by choice or by having been forced from their countries by economic or political hardship.

During session planning discussions among the authors who considered the issues discussed in the olive paper, it became clear that data to direct action is lacking. Indeed, it is difficult to know the magnitude of the problem across the United States because there is no national database documenting the location and numbers of the many immigrant populations. Problems faced by immigrants are described mainly anecdotally and are applicable only to selected immigrant or refugee groups, such as the Hmong in Minnesota or Mexicans in California.

Discussion among the session planners also focused attention on the general lack of awareness and interest permeating most federal and state agencies where, in some instances, current local and state efforts are actively discriminating against immigrants and immigration. Clearly, while little national action is anticipated, the group believes that action is warranted.

The paucity of data and apparent lack of interest caused the session planning committee to design a session based around three key areas:

1. *Scope of the problem (local to national)*: Lack of data about, lack of awareness of, and lack of interest in immigrants and their health issues and current perceptions;

2. *Major issues in immigrant women's health:* Health care access and social and economic, psychological, physical, and environmental risk factors; and,

3. *Current action across the United States*: Local, regional, and national examples.

The goal of the session was the identification of the issues relating to immigrant women and their health and session participant discussion and recommendation of initiatives for AAN action. Participants considered action on the following questions:

1. What are the three to five major issues that immigrant women face concerning their health and that of their families?

2. How do we acquire the data—epidemiological, social, legal, political—that will provide appropriate information for action concerning the health of immigrant women—locally, statewide, regionally, nationally?

3. Based on existing data and other information, what are the priority research issues for the AAN to support and promote, now, and in the future?

4. Based on existing data and other information, what are the priority knowledge development issues for the AAN to support and promote, now, and in the future?

5. Immigrant women's health is not a top priority for national women's health initiatives in research and clinical intervention. How do we change this, especially in light of the decrease in federal funding?

6. As federal funds become more scarce, what creative strategies and programs can be implemented (locally, statewide, nationally) to bring immigrant women's health concerns and care forward? What examples of excellence already exist?

7. What key areas should the AAN focus on to establish immigrant women's health as a priority area within its own organization and in collaboration with other organizations?

MAJOR ISSUES IN IMMIGRANT WOMEN'S HEALTH

Immigrant and refugee women's health issues are complex and global. They are global because of the enormous number of people who move across national boundaries. By the end of 1994, worldwide, there were 16.3 million refugees and asylum seekers in need of protection and/or assistance and more than 3 million others in refugee-like situations (U.S Committee on Refugees 1995). Women and children comprise approximately 80 percent of refugees. The United States has been the destination for more political refugees than any other nation, although it has actually received only a fraction of the international refugees and immigrants seeking asylum—the largest number of whom have settled in developing countries, with the great majority moving within their own countries (Meissner et al. 1993). It is a fallacy to think that once a family has crossed international borders, it stays there.

This paper focuses on women of reproductive age, roughly 15 years to 45 years, who are immigrants to the United States. The focus is holistic—not merely on women as vessels for children, as was the case for the majority of women's health studies until very recently.

Immigrant women's health issues are highly complex. Immigrant women's health issues vary considerably with the amount of time they have lived in the host country(ies), social conditions at the time they arrived, and their reasons for leaving their home country(ies). Health issues also vary by demographic differences; in particular, age, education, and urban or rural origin. The magnitude of cultural difference between their countries of origin and country of resettlement—including prior exposure to the culture of the host country—has an impact on how much culture shock women experience and how long it takes them to acculturate. Women's personal resources also influence their health in the host country. For example, did they bring financial resources, are they healthy, are they flexible, are their personalities hardy? Immigrant women settle in a variety of social environments with different levels of immigrant or ethnic bias, job opportunities, access to health and welfare services, and cultural harmony.

Conceptual Frameworks

There is no single comprehensive theoretical framework of migration and health; existing frameworks include psychoanalytical, epidemiological, or sociocultural approaches. The complexity of the relationship between migration and health requires a multifactorial model. Ethnographic or longitudinal studies that address many variables in social and historical context can depict this complexity, but cultural specificity may interfere with a comprehensive theoretical framework. Useful frameworks include stress, pathogenesis/salutogenesis, transitions, and marginalization.

Stress

Migration is a stressful experience requiring accommodation, adaptation, or coping (Coelho and Ahmed 1980). Stress is an intervening variable that can appreciably increase the risk of adverse health outcomes (Cassell 1974), such as hypertension, cancer, and heart disease (Hull 1979; McKinlay 1975). Acculturative stress is a reduction in the health status of individuals that can include physical, psychological, and social aspects (Williams and Berry 1991). However, instead of examining single cause-and-effect relationships, we should focus on the dynamics of adaptation, which is more difficult to characterize but more realistic (Kasl and Berkman 1983).

Most of the literature, however, emphasizes the pathogenic influence of migration and pays little attention to people who succeed. A recent Medline search revealed that perhaps 75 percent of clinical and research articles on various refugee and immigrant groups focused on physical and psychological dysfunction, with many emphasizing posttraumatic stress disorder (PTSD) among refugees (Kinzie et al. 1984). In contrast, Aroian (1990), using Antonovsky's (1979) notion of *salutogenesis* (i.e., adaptive resources and successful coping amidst ubiquitous stressors), recommends that researchers place equal emphasis on immigrants who succeed, recognizing their strengths and coping abilities. Such immigrants are proof that interpreting stressors as challenges to be met can lead to better coping skills and personal growth.

Transitions

Transitions are periods during which change is perceived by a person or by others in a particular environment to be occurring in a person or in the environment (Chick and Meleis 1986). Immigrant and resettlement transitions are prime examples of significant changes in both person and environment over a period of time.

During periods of transition, there is often loss of support until new support systems are established. There is a sense of disequilibrium and uncertainty about the future (Schumacher and Meleis 1994). Immigrants are faced with a new society—new values, norms, and expectations—which are usually neither well-defined nor uniform. Transitions also create fear of loss of identity. Immigrants feel vulnerable, torn away from a familiar pattern and put into a setting in which they feel unprepared, emotionally and culturally (Stevens, Hall, and Meleis 1992). These feelings of uprootedness—along with needing to function in an unfamiliar environment in which the symbols have to be constantly interpreted—cause distress. This distress is often manifested in depression and somatic complaints (Mirdal 1984). Transitions are also cumulative. If issues related to life transitions are not resolved, they can be aggravated when immigrants face other transitions in their lives—for example, the postpartum transition or a chronic illness.

Marginalization and Health

Immigrant women are more vulnerable because they are marginalized. Hall, Stevens, and Meleis (1994) define marginalization as (a) person(s) being distinguished from the norm in a situation with negative attribution associated with being different. Margins are defined as "the peripheral, boundary-determining aspects of persons, social networks, communities, and environments" (Hall, Stevens, and Meleis 1994). Immigrant women share the situation of being marginal with impoverished women and women of color. Their accents or appearance often set them apart in the eyes of people of the dominant culture, who may express anything from mild disrespect to virulent prejudice. Marginalized people lack power in many realms. In other realms, their power is not appreciated or understood by the majority of people (Meleis, Lipson, and Muecke, in press).

Seeking out health and social services, marginalized people tend to guard information that may expose their differences or further marginalize them, disclosing personal information only to those they trust. They face many types of institutional barriers to health care. Marginalization is created and enforced by societal values, which in turn influence the philosophy upon which health care systems are built. These systems tend to perpetuate these myths and stereotypes (Meleis, Lipson, and Muecke 1995).

Definitions and Numbers

Immigration has been defined as the movement of persons from one country to another with the intention of permanent residence. *Migration* has been defined as movement within the same country. But the terms are becoming conceptually blurred in the literature and are often used interchangeably. The U.S. Immigration and Naturalization Service (INS) defines an immigrant as a nonresident alien admitted for permanent residence. In contrast, a *refugee* is someone who is admitted outside normal quota restrictions because he or she has a well-founded fear of persecution because of his or her race, religion, nationality, social group, or political opinion. An *asylum seeker* is a person who has come to the United States applying for *refugee* status. *Illegal alien*, a term with negative connotations, means someone who is "undocumented," a person who does not possess documents allowing him or her to reside in the United States.

The hierarchy of preferences for admitting immigrants and refugees is spelled out by the INS, but the number of people admitted from any one nation is influenced by the U.S. Government's political relationship with that specific nation. For example, for many years, Central Americans were not admitted as refugees to the United States despite the probability that the majority would have been classified as refugees because they fled their home countries in fear for their lives.

The highest priority is accorded immigrants to the United States who are determined to be in immediate danger of loss of their lives or political prisoners referred to the United Nations High Commissioner for Refugees (UNHCR) or a U.S. embassy, and vulnerable cases, such as women at risk and torture survivors. The largest number in this category are of special concern because of nationality—for example, for Fiscal Year 1995, persons from Burma, Laos, Vietnam, the former Soviet Union, Bosnia, Cuba, Haiti, and Iran. Of next highest priority are immediate relatives of persons lawfully admitted as permanent resident aliens, refugees, or asylees; unmarried children of U.S. citizens; and parents of U.S. citizens under 21 years old. Next in priority are more distant relatives of those admitted under higher priority levels.

The largest numbers of immigrants to the United States came during 1900-1920 (9 million) and 1980-1990 (10 million). The percentage of foreign-born U.S. residents has ranged from 15 percent at the turn of the century to less than 9 percent today. Currently, there are about 22 million foreign-born residents in the United States. In 1993, there were 800,000 legal immigrants, 66 percent coming for family reunification with permanent residents of the United States. Fifteen percent were admitted as political refugees, 15 percent were brought in for their special skills, and the rest were admitted as special cases. More than 75 percent of all immigrants live in California, New York, Texas, Florida, New Jersey, and Illinois.

The INS estimates that there are some 2 million to 3 million undocumented immigrants, about 1.5 percent of the total population, which is only about 15 percent of the foreign-born population. However, the American public appears to believe that most immigrants come to the United States illegally. In September 1994, there was a backlog of 600,000 asylum cases awaiting decisions. Recent immigration reform is attempting to speed up "processing" people by expediting procedures for asylum seekers arriving at airports with missing or fraudulent documents. In the past 15 years, the Office of Refugee Resettlement reduced refugee cash and medical assistance from three years to five months, which is insufficient time for refugees to learn English and become economically self-sufficient.

The upsurge in anti-immigrant sentiment is largely an outgrowth of recession and high unemployment. The current backlash, exploited by many politicians in the last few years, tends to portray newcomers as a drag on the economy. New arrivals are seen as competing for scarce jobs and worsening local and state budget problems by requiring tax-supported services. However, a 1994 California State Senate Office of Research study found that the foreign-born who came to California between 1980 and 1990 were not much more likely to receive public assistance than the general population (4.8 percent versus 4.1 percent), even though their median annual household income was much lower ($22,300 versus $34,900). Because recent immigrants to California are younger, only 1.5 percent draw Social Security benefits compared to 13 percent of long-term Californians. While they fill the schools, their parents generally pay taxes which help to support the schools as well as supporting Social Security for native-born recipients. They mainly vie for jobs with other immigrants for tough work at low pay.

A FRAMEWORK FOR EXAMINING MAJOR ISSUES
IN IMMIGRANT WOMEN'S HEALTH

There are a number of ways to categorize influences on the health of women immigrants. For example, Afghan refugees in the United States experience three types of stressors: 1) the traumas people faced in Afghanistan, such as having observed atrocities, imprisonment/torture of self or family members, difficult escapes, and loss of family, property, culture, and social status; 2) current daily concerns engendered by news and infor-mation from Afghanistan; and, 3) current resettlement and adjustment issues in U.S. society (Lipson and Omidian, in press, Western Journal of Nursing Research).

For the purposes of this session, we have divided stressors into five major areas: 1) social risk factors, 2) psychological risk factors, 3) physical risk factors, 4) environmental risk factors, and 5) health care access problems. Obviously, there is a great deal of overlap and interaction between and among these issues, and different risk factors are highlighted for different women. In listing risk factors, we do not want to emphasize only risks or pathology. Women vary in their strength and coping mechanisms, and many come out stronger through coping effectively with these stressors.

Social Risk Factors

Immigrant women often are overloaded with multiple roles and responsibilities. Because of economic need, many have two jobs; they are also homemakers and many care for other relatives. In one example, a woman was responsible for accompanying her brother to the local department of motor vehicles to help him get his driver's license because he could not speak English, making a doctor's appointment and interpreting for her sister, doing the paperwork to sponsor her eldest sister's immigration to the United States, and taking care of her when she arrived. This woman works in a restaurant making salads for minimum wage, cooks the family meals, and does all the housework. If a woman is the only family member who drives, she may not be able to keep a job because she cannot refuse when family members ask her to drive them to appointments and school.

Jobs with low pay and no benefits

Immigrant women often work in oppressive situations and environments. They tend to be in dead-end, low status, and low prestige occupations, and often work triple shifts daily (Lipson and Miller 1994; Weitzman and Berry 1992). They are often more able and willing than their husbands to take such jobs as fast food clerk, domestic worker, hotel maid, or family-owned small grocery store attendant. In some instances, they have limited control over the money they earn. Their work is not reflected in statistics, and they are considered non-productive (Meleis, Lipson and Muecke, in press).

Poverty and lack of education

Education among women immigrants varies widely, but in many of the countries from which the women originate, girls have less access to education than boys. In some refugee groups, such as Afghans and the Hmong, older women may have had no education at all. In general, refugees who were professionals in their own countries become downwardly mobile and rarely regain their former social status. Other families improve their economic situation in the United States, usually because everyone in the family is working very hard at two or more jobs.

But the women often do not have access to the money they earn; even if the woman is the main wage earner, her check goes to the family. Many immigrant women lack financial security and governmental support. Relevant questions include: What kind of governmental support should immigrants or refugees receive? What other kinds of assistance—training, English classes, money? Does financial support or welfare reinforce dependency?

Language

Inadequate fluency in English is one of the strongest barriers to immigrant integration into U.S. society. It blocks communication with neighbors, prevents immigrants from learning the "rules" and easier ways to meet their everyday needs, and keeps them from better paying jobs. Some immigrant women speak adequate, if accented, English but do not read or write it.

Lack of social support, isolation

Immigrant women with children at home are often very isolated and lonely. Many do not live near immigrants from their home country, and they may not be able to speak enough English to relate to neighbors. In patriarchal societies, husbands may insist that they not leave the house. Their former social support systems, consisting of female relatives and other extended family members, neighbors, and old friends, are not available, and they cannot socialize in the customary way. Many women describe missing most the opportunity to drop in on each other daily, which they often cannot do in the United States where there is little available leisure time for informal socializing.

Ethnic bias, public and statutory xenophobia

Immigrants suffer because of unfriendly neighbors and outright hostility in their immediate communities. They are frustrated and saddened by constant reminders that they do not belong, making their integration into the mainstream even more difficult (Hattar-Pollara and Meleis 1995). Immigrants feel stereotyped, misunderstood, and set apart.

Bias is a source of stress. The general public does not discriminate among a legally admitted refugee or immigrant, an undocumented person, or an American citizen with an accent and dark skin. Everyone who was born elsewhere must bear the brunt of the current anti-immigrant wave. Legislation and initiatives like California's Proposition 187 promote visible discrimination. Newcomers, not understanding that they are entitled to such services, may be afraid to seek health care, even when they have appropriate documents.

Risks for undocumented women

Undocumented women experience legitimate paranoia; they limit their activities for fear of discovery and deportation, only seeking health care in acute crisis. They are at risk for spousal abuse, health problems, poverty, and many other problems (DeSantis 1990).

Psychological Risk Factors

Loss

In addition to their country and culture, immigrant women have often lost family members and property. Many experience an undercurrent of unresolved grief attached to their losses, particularly refugees who have experienced many such losses and would not have chosen to leave their homes if they had a choice.

Posttraumatic stress disorder (PTSD)

PTSD is a serious health outcome of refugee flight. Many refugee women who seek health care do so for symptoms of PTSD, such as nightmares, sleep disorders, and somatic complaints. Psychological complaints include depression, withdrawal, avoidance, loneliness, persecution reactions, apathy, hopelessness, death/dying themes, loss of self-confidence (Boehnlein 1987; Kinzie et al. 1984; Shepard and Faust 1993), reexperiencing the traumatic event, and numbing of responsiveness to—or reduced involvement with—the external world. PTSD can be chronic and last several years or emerge after a long delay. It is frequently misdiagnosed.

Home country conflict

Many health providers rarely recognize the impact of ongoing preoccupation with home among immigrants from war-torn countries; they cannot imagine the power of the news and the worry about relatives who remain. Frequently, immigrants' mood, stress levels, and symptoms change as the news changes, sometimes on a daily basis when they come from countries that are highly unstable politically. The concept of transnationalism—a social phenomenon in which migrants maintain relationships across political, cultural, and geographical boundaries—is very important when considering the situation of immigrant women who are strongly tied to home through events and visits back and forth (Lipson and Omidian 1996).

Culture conflict

This stressor is a common issue for immigrant women; the work of managing daily life with inadequate English, money, and transportation makes life even more difficult. Those of us who have lived in other countries will remember our initial exhaustion from just attempting to function effectively from day to day, even if we knew the language. A more subtle dilemma is the conflict between the North American value of individualism and individual rights and the collectivist cultures from which many immigrants come. The very fabric of Euro-American life is woven of individual choices and rights, which confuses women who have a difficult time perceiving themselves as individuals and who, instead, see themselves as family members. Being asked to make decisions for themselves in health care when they expect their family to make this decision illustrates this conflict.

Family role change

In some immigrant groups, women seem to acculturate more quickly than men do; the women become caught between the immigrant community's expectations that they behave traditionally and their desire for American-style freedom and independence. Because women often get jobs more easily than their spouses can, there may be family conflict when the husband is not working. Disturbing the traditional patriarchal role can cause marital problems.

Children acculturate much more rapidly than their parents do; they come home from school asserting their individual rights learned from teachers and peers. Women are often more tolerant of their children's acculturation than are men. The women are the "culture brokers," the family mediators between husband and children, children and school, and perhaps other relatives and social and health care agencies. They are the ones who integrate the family into the new culture and yet they are expected to maintain their cultural heritage and its values and norms (Meleis 1991; Hattar-Pollara and Meleis 1995).

Domestic violence

Although we know that family violence crosses cultural, economic, and educational lines, we have little trustworthy hard data on its prevalence among immigrant women. A current study being conducted by Ayuda, a domestic violence program for Latina women, is finding that 60 percent of undocumented Latina women have been battered by their intimate partners, and 77 percent married to U.S. citizens and permanent residents batter their partners (National Council for Research on Women 1995).

We have little knowledge of interventions that might be culturally sensitive. For example, women might ask whether or not it is easier to find ways to live with the violence than to escape to homelessness. These are areas of needed research (Frye and D'Avanzo 1994). We do know that many patriarchal cultures condone husbands "disciplining" their wives when they are not properly submissive. We also know that many immigrant husbands' self-esteem is shattered by their inability to obtain a decent job or any job at all or to perform their accustomed roles of supporting the family and representing it to the outside world. These men may become very depressed and angry and abuse drugs or alcohol, behavior which may be related to abusing their wives and children.

Most immigrant women, regardless of their legal status, fear the American legal system. Even documented women often believe that reporting domestic violence can lead to their deportation. In many cases, the batterer never filed immigration papers for his immigrant spouse, and many batterers use immigration law as a tool to hold their wives and children in violent homes. In many immigrant groups it is culturally unacceptable to divulge such private information as that concerning family relationships to an outsider. Across many cultures, however, women's shame and feeling that they may be responsible is extremely common.

Physical Risk Factors

Pathogens from home or transit countries

Immigrants have higher rates of tuberculosis and hepatitis B than the general population in the United States (CDC 1990). They may arrive with parasitic diseases, such as schistosomiasis, that are not readily recognized in primary care. Genetic problems also may not be recognized, like the Glucose-6-phosphate dehydrogenase deficiency or thalassemia which is common in Mediterranean people and which causes anemia.

Numerous pregnancies

Many immigrant women have married very young and have borne many children. Because numerous pregnancies cause wear and tear on women's bodies, immigrant women in their 40s may appear to be much older than their chronological age. For example, prolapsed uterus is more common at a young age.

Poor past nutritional status

Many immigrants, and immigrant women in particular, suffer from poor nutrition associated with poverty, long stays in refugee camps, or being from countries in which men and children are always served first. Current nutritional status may be negatively affected by a high sugar, fat, and salt fast-food diet, or food preparation methods that are unhealthy, such as using excessive oil or overcooking vegetables.

Specific practices

Some immigrant women are from countries in which specific practices can pose health risks—for example, female circumcision or chewing betel nuts, which leads to gum and tooth damage. Health providers may not recognize such practices or may react to them negatively, further traumatizing the women.

Poor prevention, health promotion practices

Many immigrant women rarely engage in adequate physical activity. Many factors interfere—lack of knowledge of the importance of physical activity to one's health, work/family responsibilities that allow no time for self-enhancing activities, transportation or financial problems, modesty, and cultural viewpoints about the inappropriateness of exercise for women. Diet, however, is much more commonly regarded as part of health promotion, and this is an area where women immigrants can change and reduce their own health risks and those of their family members.

Environmental Risk Factors

Neighborhood violence

In some areas in which new immigrants and refugees settle, poverty, drugs, and gangs are part of everyday life. For example, in some neighborhoods, women and children remain imprisoned in their houses for safety all day until the father or adult sons come home to take them out.

Poor housing

Immigrant women who live in impoverished neighborhoods often live in polluted environments where they encounter such hazards as exposure to lead in paint or traffic and industrial pollutants. Their houses may be inadequately insulated and they may face other environmental hazards associated with poor housing.

Work site hazards

Work site hazards include long hours or environmental conditions that increase health risks. Many immigrant women are taken advantage of because only a few jobs are available to them. For example, a recent San Francisco newspaper article described a group of Thai women who had been promised good jobs if they came to the United States; however, when they arrived, they were imprisoned in a local sweatshop, worked for seven days a week for almost no money and were threatened with arrest and deportation if they complained to anyone.

Health Care Risks

Legislation

There has been considerable fallout from California's Proposition 187 and its counterparts in terms of psychological effects on immigrants, particularly in California but elsewhere as well. In California, it is still common for many permanent and legal residents to avoid seeking health care because they misunderstand the implications of this legislation or do not know that it has not yet been implemented. Others are afraid of being suspected, discriminated against, or provided poor quality care because they think that health care providers work for the INS. If implemented, this kind of legislation has many implications for nurses. For example, how will nurses know who is not a legal resident? Should nurses be placed in the position of acting as police?

No insurance/financial barriers

Not having enough money to pay for health care is a barrier common to poor or minority women in general. Some refugee/immigrant populations had access to Medicaid, but in some areas, many physicians no longer accept it; in other areas, conversion of Medicaid to HMOs or managed care has effectively blocked access for immigrant women. Following is a discussion of some of the reasons.

Language barriers

Not being able to speak or understand English is a major barrier to obtaining health care. A quote from an Afghan woman describes this dilemma well: "It's very hard to get to the doctor. One person has to find the right kind of doctor and one who takes Medi-Cal. Another person has to make the appointment. One has to drive us there. One has to translate" (Lipson and Omidian 1992). The use of family members as interpreters has many drawbacks; often, a child is the only family member who speaks enough English but, at the same time, he or she does not have the maturity or vocabulary to interpret adequately. Picture a 12-year-old boy from a strongly modest culture with social separation of men and women being asked to interpret for his mother at an appointment with a gynecologist. Often, interpreter children or family members withhold from health providers information that may show a parent in a negative light. Gender matching is important in many cultures.

Transportation and child care

These issues, as well as the last two, are common to poor women of any background. Women who do not drive, have no car, or live in areas in which public transportation is poor or unsafe have difficulty getting to medical care. The inability to afford child care also decreases access.

Clinic structure/hours

Many immigrant women cannot obtain health care because clinic hours are the same as working hours, or long waits preclude being able to be seen during a lunch hour. They may be at risk of losing their jobs if they take time off when ill or seek care for themselves or family members.

Health providers' lack of knowledge

Health providers from the dominant culture often do not understand immigrant women's experiences, explanatory frameworks of illness, or communication patterns. Examples include victims of torture or war who experience PTSD or other symptoms related to what they have experienced, or immigrant patients who use different ways of describing the body. For example, telling a health provider that "my kidney is hot."

GROUP DISCUSSION

More than 50 Academy members attended the session. Although the olive paper had been distributed at the beginning of the session, there wasn't adequate time to review and absorb its content before the session commenced. Therefore, Lipson's presentation offered a synthesis of issues and a suggested framework for viewing the health care of immigrant women to serve as the basis for the discussion and decisions requested of Academy members.

After general discussion by the whole group of participants, four small groups met to consider two of the seven questions introduced by Judith LaRosa, Ph.D., F.A.A.N.:

- What are the three to five major issues immigrant women face in their health and the health of their families?

- How do we acquire the data (epidemiological, social, and legal) which will provide appropriate information for health actions concerning immigrant women and their health?

After small-group discussions, the full session met again to identify key areas on which the AAN should focus to establish immigrant women's health as a priority area within the organization and in collaboration with other organizations.

An outcome of the lively small-group discussions was that the group as a whole was divided on whether to label women who have immigrated to the United States as "immigrants" at all. Given the current political climate, there was concern that such a label would be divisive. Instead, some members asked that the topic be framed more generally as issues in the health care of vulnerable women and their families. Outside of culture-specific health issues and language barriers, several people expressed the belief that immigrant women face health care issues common to all women who are considered vulnerable for a variety of reasons.

Session participants reached consensus on four key concerns for Academy consideration in developing future action plans:

1. Develop national databases on immigrant women, databases which are essential to furthering our efforts to describe existing communities and work toward policy and legislative agendas appropriate to specific communities and their assets.

2. Promote the establishment of community partnerships modeled on the framework of primary health care and dedicated to bringing community and professional participants together to develop a holistic model of health care.

3. Ensure collaboration between major nursing organizations (AAN, ANA, and ICN) and governmental and private and public health officials in addressing issues relative to migration, immigration, international humanitarian aid, and refugee status, issues that are important to immigrant women.

4. Pursue legislation that mandates mechanisms to ensure that immigrant women can communicate about their health care in a preferred language.

While it is still early in the process of determining AAN consensus on future action items, the concerns raised by Academy members regarding the health care of women immigrants become more compelling each day. Their care is a special challenge in the large cities to which so many of them have migrated. In essence, our action to ensure essential health care and access to that care for immigrant women is an act of political will required of health professionals and organizations that aspire to the provision of care and humanitarian aid.

REFERENCES

Antonovsky, A. 1979. *Health, stress and coping.* San Francisco: Jossey-Bass Publishers.

Aroian, K.J. 1990. A model of psychological adaptation to migration and resettlement. *Nursing Research* 39(1): 5-10.

Boehnlein, J.K. 1987. Clinical relevance of grief and mourning among Cambodian refugees. *Social Science and Medicine* 25: 765-772.

Cassell, J. 1974. Psychosocial processes and stress: Theoretical formulation. *International Journal of Health Services* 4: 471-481.

Centers for Disease Control and Prevention, Public Health Service, U.S. Department of Health and Human Services. 1990. Tuberculosis among foreign-born persons entering the United States: Recommendations of the Advisory Council for the Elimination of Tuberculosis. *Morbidity and Mortality Weekly Report* 39: RR-18, 28.

Chick, N., and Meleis, A.I. 1986. Transitions: A nursing concern. In *Nursing research methodology*, P.L. Chinn, ed., pp. 237-257. Boulder, CO: Aspen Publishers.

Coelho C., and Ahmed, P., eds. 1980. *Uprooting and development*. New York: Plenum.

DeSantis, L. 1990. Fieldwork with undocumented aliens and other populations at risk. *Western Journal of Nursing Research* 12(3): 359-372.

Frye, B.A., and D'Avanzo, C.D. 1994. Cultural themes in family stress and violence among Cambodian refugee women in the inner city. *Advances in Nursing Science* 16(3): 64-77.

Hall, J.A., Stevens, P.E., and Meleis, A.I. 1994. Marginalization: A guiding concept for valuing diversity in nursing knowledge development. *Advances in Nursing Science* 16(4): 23-41.

Hattar-Pollara, M., and Meleis, A.I. 1995. The daily lived experiences of Jordanian immigrant women in the United States. *Western Journal of Nursing Research* 17: 521-538.

Hull, D. 1979. Migration, adaptation and illness: A review. *Social Science and Medicine* 13A: 25-36.

Kasl, S.V., and Berkman, L. 1983. Health consequences of the experience of migration. *Annual Review of Public Health* 4: 69-90.

Kinzie, J.D., Fredrickson, R.H., Ben, R., Fleck, J., and Karis, W. 1984. Posttraumatic stress disorder among survivors of Cambodian concentration camps. *American Journal of Psychiatry* 141(5): 645-650.

Lipson, J,. and Miller, S. 1994. Changing roles of Afghan refugee women in the U.S. *Health Care for Women International* 15: 171-180.

Lipson, J.G., and Omidian, P. 1992. Afghan refugees: Health issues in the United States. *Western Journal of Medicine* 157(3): 271-275.

°°°. 1996. Health and the transnational connection: Afghan refugees in the United States. In *CORI Selected Papers on Refugee Issues* IV:1-16, A. Rynearson and J. Phillips, eds.,VA: American Anthropological Association.

°°°. (in press) Afghan refugee issues in the U.S. social environment. *Western Journal of Nursing Research*.

McKinlay, J. 1975. Some issues associated with migration, health status, and the use of human services. *Journal of Chronic Disease* 28:579-592.

Meissner, D., Hormats, R., Walker,, A., and Ogata, S. 1993. Migration challenges in a new era: A report to the Trilateral Commission. New York.

Meleis, A. I. l991. Between two cultures: Identity, roles and health. *Health Care for Women International* 12: 365-378.

Meleis, A.I., Lipson, J., and Muecke, M. (In press). Immigrant women and their health: Time to take heed. An olive paper.

Mirdal, G. M. 1984. Stress and distress in migration: Problems and resources of Turkish women in Denmark. *International Migration Review* 18: 984-1003.

National Council for Research On Women. 1995. Intervening: Immigrant women and domestic violence. *Issues Quarterly* 1(3): 12-13.

Shepard, J., and Faust, S. 1993. Refugee health care and the problem of suffering. *Bioethics Forum* 9(3): 3-7.

Schumacher, K., and Meleis, A. 1994. Transitions: A central concept in nursing. *Image* 26(2): 119-127.

Stevens, P., Hall, J., and Meleis, A. 1992. Examining vulnerability of women clerical workers from five ethnic/racial groups. *Western Journal of Nursing Research* 14: 754-774.

U.S. Committee for Refugees 1995. *World refugee survey - 1995.* New York: Immigration and Refugee Services of America.

Weitzman, B. C., and Berry, C. A. 1992. Health status and health care utilization among New York City home attendants: An illustration of needs of working poor, immigrant women. *Women and Health* 19(2/3): 87-105.

Williams, C., and Berry, J. 1991. Primary prevention of acculturative stress among refugees: Application of psychological theory and practice. *American Psychologist* 46: 632-641.

Selected Resources on Immigrants and Refugees

Publications: Journals

Journal of Refugee Studies
Quarterly, research, programs, subscription
Oxford University Press
Walton Street
Oxford OX2 6DP
United Kingdom
44(0)1865 56767
FAX: 44(0) 1865 267782
(send orders and sample copy requests to Journals Subscriptions Department)

International Migration Review
Quarterly, research, programs, subscription
Center for Migration Studies of New York, Inc.
209 Flagg Place
Staten Island, NY 10304-1199
(718) 351-8800
FAX (718) 667-4598

Refugees
Monthly, programs, news, free
United Nations High Commissioner for Refugees
P.O. Box 2500
CH 1211, Geneva 2 Depot
Switzerland
(022) 739-81 11
FAX (public information) (022) 739 84-49

Refugee Reports
Monthly, statistics, news, subscription
U.S. Committee for Refugees News Service
1717 Massachusetts Ave., NW, Suite 701
Washington, DC 20036
Subscriptions: Sunbelt Fulfillment Services
P.O. Box 5026
Brentwood, TN 37024
(615) 377-3322

Migration and Health
Quarterly, newsletter, free
International Organization for Migration (IOM)
17 Route Des Morillons
CH-1211 Geneva 19
Switzerland

Migration and Mental Health Newsletter
Newsletter, free
Wissenschaftliches Institut der Arzte Deutschlands e.V. (WIAD)
Godesberger Allee 54
D-53175 Bonn, Germany
49-228-8104-172
FAX: 49-228-8104-155

Publications: Books and Reports

Refugee Women, UNHCR (UN High Commissioner for Refugees), No. 100, II.
UNHCR
1775 K St., NW, #300
Washington, DC 20006

From Nairobi to Beijing: Report of the Secretary General
New York: The United Nations 1995
Sales No. E.95.IV.5

The United Nations and the Advancement of Women: 1945-1995
New York: The United Nations Blue Book Series 1995
Sales No. 95.1.29

The World's Women 1995: Trends and Statistics
New York: The United Nations
Sales No. E.95.XVII.2

Women: Looking beyond 2000
New York: The United Nations 1995
Sales No. E.95.I.40

Organizations

National Council for International Health (NCIH)
1701 K Street NW, Suite 600
Washington, DC 20006
(292) 833-5900
FAX (202) 833-0075

U.S. Committee for Refugees
1717 Massachusetts Ave., NW, Suite 701
Washington, DC 20036
(202) 347-3507
FAX: (202) 347-3418

Amnesty International, USA
322 Eighth Ave.
New York, NY 10001

InterAction
1717 Massachusetts Ave, NW, Suite 801
Washington, DC 20036
(202) 667-8236

Women's Environment and Development Organization (WEDO)
845 Third Ave, 15th Floor
New York, NY 10022
(212) 759-7982

Electronic (Web sites)

U.S. Census Bureau: www.census.gov

Charlotte's Web (immigrant issues papers):
stp://heather.cs.ucdavis.edu/pub/Immigration/Index/html

Emerging Infectious Diseases: Symptoms of Global Change

PAUL R. EPSTEIN, M.D., M.P.H.
Department of Medicine
Harvard Medical School

FELISSA L. COHEN, PH.D., R.N., F.A.A.N.
Dean, School of Nursing
Southern Illinois University

ELAINE LARSON, PH.D., R.N., F.A.A.N.
Dean, School of Nursing
Georgetown University

INTRODUCTION

The 1995 Annual Meeting of the American Academy of Nursing (AAN) concurrent session on the topic of "Emerging Microbes" had three principal objectives: to discuss reemergence of microbes in the world and the role played by immigration; to explain facts and statistics on reemerging microbes; and to discuss how global transport, environmental changes, and population movements enhance opportunities for infectious diseases (i.e., the relationship among climate, ecology, and public health). Session participants developed recommendations for nursing and for the Academy with regard to emerging infectious diseases, those "infections that have newly appeared in a population or have existed but are rapidly increasing in incidence or geographic range" (Morse 1995).

Reemerging diseases also are a problem. Reemergence refers to the reappearance of a known disease that had previously declined in incidence or was thought to be under control (Moran et al. 1995). Table 1 lists some examples of emerging infectious diseases.

A focus of the Academy session was the extent to which the epidemiology and redistribution or reemergence of infectious diseases is associated with modification of social and political systems and environmental change. Efforts to improve economic productivity or quality of life can inadvertently result in changes in the reservoirs or vectors of infection or the microorganisms themselves, increasing risk to human hosts.

The significant increase in schistosomiasis and Rift Valley fever with the building of dams in Africa (Jouan et al. 1989; Shope and Evans 1993), the rapid emergence of multiple-drug resistant (MDR) strains of microorganisms with increasing environmental and clinical use of antibiotics (Kunin 1993; Spratt 1993), and the emergence of Argentine hemorrhagic fever associated with changes in the flora (i.e., tall grasses) and fauna (i.e., proliferation of the mouse reservoir and killing off of cats) as a result of herbicide use (Garrett 1994) are examples of the actual and potential negative effects of environmental manipulation.

GLOBAL DISTRIBUTION OF INFECTIOUS DISEASES

The Centers for Disease Control and Prevention (CDC), World Health Organization (WHO), and the United States Department of State are concerned that infectious diseases are emerging, resurgent, and undergoing redistribution at an accelerating rate.

The resurgence or redistribution of emerging infectious diseases may be one of the first symptoms of global change. Global change is defined as: 1) climate change; 2) decreased stratospheric ozone; and, 3) widespread ecological change (e.g., deforestation) affecting the global systems. Some infectious diseases (like pertussis) are directly transmitted (person to person); others (like malaria and dengue fever) involve several species and thus respond more to ecological and climactic factors. Rodent-borne diseases (e.g., hantavirus, leptospirosis, plague), for example, are encouraged by prolonged droughts (which reduce the number of predators) punctuated by torrential rains (which provide food sources). In the marine environment, multiple factors favor the overgrowth of coastal plankton blooms, the reservoir for cholera bacteria.

CLIMATE AND DISEASE

Many connections between the physical environment and biological phenomena were clear to malaria researchers in the 1920s. Temperature and precipitation anomalies are correlated with outbreaks of malaria and temperature is related to insect generation time, insect size, insect biting rates and longevity, and to parasite incubation. Paleoclimatic data demonstrate that past warm periods were associated with rapid redistribution of insect fauna.

Growing understanding of the climate system allows even greater inferences concerning climate patterns and vector-borne diseases (VBDs). Algae and zooplankton, like terrestrial insect vectors, respond to warming (given adequate nutrients) with accelerated photosynthesis and metabolism, and warming and stratification of the water column favor a shift in species composition toward the more toxic cyanobacteria and dinoflagellates.

The distribution of disease vectors is affected by long-term climate trends, while variability and extreme events (e.g., droughts and floods) generate new breeding ground and new bursts of activity. As the latter are often connected to the El Nino phenomenon (i.e., anomalous warming in the Eastern Pacific Ocean), improvements in *climate forecasting* and connections to weather events across the globe can contribute to early warning systems for timely, environmentally sound public health interventions.

Ecology and Disease

Ecologists describe opportunistic species as those exhibiting r-selection—i.e., having high *reproductive* rates. R-selected species—weeds, insects, rodents, fungi, protozoa, bacteria, and viruses—have small body size, huge broods, rapid generation times, and good dispersal mechanisms. They are "generalists" with wide-ranging appetites, and excellent colonizers of new environments.

Those exhibiting *K*-selection have larger bodies, reproduce later in life, and produce small broods. *K* represents the environmental carrying capacity for species whose growth becomes limited as its population increases. *K*-selected species are "specialists" but are superior competitors in stable environments, keeping rs in check (what is known as biological control).

In perturbed environments (or weakened hosts) r-selected species rapidly assume dominance. The growth of opportunistic *rs*—the pests, parasites, and pathogens—is thus encouraged in 1) monocultures (i.e., those environments devoid of genetic and species diversity), 2) where pesticides eliminate large predators, 3) where habitat is fragmented, *and*, 4) when climate change disturbs synchronies among species.

Warming itself increases the generation—and can accelerate the evolution—of *r* species, given their rapid reproductive rates. *R*-selected species are now increasing in terrestrial and marine systems, across a wide range of taxonomic groups, as regulatory (defensive) systems are weakened by multiple stresses. A morbillivirus (measles family), for example, is killing Australian horses, Serengeti lions, and sea mammals in the northern and southern hemispheres. What environmental factors in each setting are decreasing host immunity?

The Intergovernmental Panel on Climate Change (IPCC) and Physical Indicators of Climate Change

The Intergovernmental Panel on Climate Change Working Group I models future climates and assesses current observations to detect the "fingerprints" of climate change. Some physical indications of a warming trend include:

- deep warming of three tropical oceans and warming waters around both poles;

- more frequent and prolonged El Nino events (the 1990-1995 anomaly is a 1 in 2,000-year event—since 1877, no El Nino event has persisted for longer than three years);

- a sea level rise;

- changes in land temperatures;

- the disproportionate rise of minimum temperatures (nighttime and winter), frost being critical for insect survival;

- melting of tropical mountain glaciers on six continents; and,

- the upward shift of height at which freezing occurs in the mountains (from 60 meters to 80 meters or upward shift of .5 degrees centigrade per decade for the past two decades).

Biological Indication

Biological evidence of long-term climate change involves the redistribution of insect vectors and of plants. *Aedes aegypti* (carrier of yellow fever and dengue ["breakbone"] fever) began to spread in the Americas in the 1980s and in 1995 blanketed the continent. This mosquito is being found at higher altitudes in several nations. Malaria vectors are found at higher altitudes in Africa and at higher latitudes than previously (Houston, Texas; New Jersey [1991] and New York [1993]), and the seasonality is extending in South America.

Plants have been reported to be migrating upward in the Swiss Alps, New Zealand, Alaska, and the Sierra Nevadas in the United States.

The El Nino Phenomena

El Nino/Southern Oscillation (ENSO) events affect weather patterns throughout the world, changing temperature and water distribution, and, thus, agriculture, hydroelectric power, and human health. Specific regions of the earth experience droughts or floods in a pattern that has been repeated regularly since ENSO records were begun in 1877.

Outbreaks of malaria, eastern equine encephalitis (in the northeast United States), waterborne gastroenteritis (e.g., salmonella in Chile and Peru), and new appearances of harmful algal blooms (in Asia and North America)—all show correlations with El Nino events. Additionally, cholera bacteria attach to algae and animal plankton, and resurgences of cholera in Bangladesh since the 1960s and the 1991 outbreak in South America have been associated with surges of algal blooms and ENSO events.

Four atmospheric-oceanic general circulation models (AOGCMs) predict that ENSO events will become more frequent with climate change. The increase in the frequency, intensity, and duration of ENSOs—and related biological events since 1976—suggest that this trend may have begun.

Climate Variability

Evidence from midwestern grain yields indicates that warming periods may be associated with increased climate variability. The warming periods from 1900 to 1940, and 1970 to the present, are associated with high variability, whereas the cooling period between 1940 and 1970 shows less oscillation around the mean conditions.

Recent work by the National Climactic Data Center (part of the U.S. National Oceanic and Atmospheric Administration [NOAA]) found increased extreme events (e.g., prolonged droughts, intense rains) in the United States since 1980.

Climactic variability and instability in the past (based on Greenland ice-core records) accompanied the large jump in temperature 10,000 years ago, heralding the current Holocene climate regime in which ice caps receded in the Northern Hemisphere and agriculture and our current civilization flourished.

RODENT-BORNE DISEASES

El Nino events and the cumulative effects of year-to-year variability (e.g., prolonged droughts) affect ecosystem dynamics, with the impacts cascading through the community of species. The six-year California drought followed by heavy 1993 rains set the stage for spreading fires. Similarly, six years of drought in the southwestern United States (and in southern Africa), followed by heavy rains in 1993, increased rodent food sources, and at the same time reduced rodent predators (i.e., owls, coyotes, and snakes). Without predators and well-nourished, the rodents flourished, increasing their numbers tenfold.

In the United States, a "new" disease, the hantavirus (with over 50 percent mortality), emerged in the Four Corners area of Arizona, New Mexico, Colorado, and Utah. In southern Africa, rodents consumed growing and stored grain and compromised food supplies. Later, an epidemic of plague emerged. In India, a plague outbreak (involving rodents and fleas) followed a 124-degree Fahrenheit summer that left animal carcasses dotting the countryside. The ensuing unusually heavy monsoons (biennially related to El Nino events) crowded humans, rodents, and insects in Surat(in northwest India), precipitating pneumonic plague, plus upsurges in dengue fever and malaria.

ARE EMERGING INFECTIOUS DISEASES A NEW PHENOMENON?

By the end of the 1960s, control of infectious disease was thought to be in sight. The 1970s were quiet years for infections, and the public health field turned its attention to chronic diseases.

Major historical transitions have been associated with diseases occurring over large areas, with such pandemics having great impacts on civilizations. Large plague pandemics occurred as the Roman Empire collapsed (541 A.D.), for example, and again at the depths of the Middle Ages (1346 A.D.). Mid-19th century Dickensian cities were beset by cholera, smallpox, and tuberculosis (TB). Have we entered a period of social and ecological vulnerability, such as these, compounded by accelerated climate change?

FUTURE SCENARIOS

Based on ecological thresholds for insect development, the boundaries for malaria and dengue fever are projected to continue to shift. RIVM (The Netherlands Department of Public Health) projects that North America and northern Europe will have bioclimatic conditions *conducive* to maintaining malaria (and dengue fever), and that more than a million additional people worldwide may die annually as a result of the impact of climate change on malaria transmission. While malaria transmission now occurs over 41.5 percent of the land surface of the globe, that figure could rise to 60 percent with a doubling of greenhouse gases.

COSTS OF DISEASE EVENTS

The costs of epidemics can be enormous. Beyond the illnesses and deaths, there are losses in work productivity, and land unused because of the presence of disease vectors. Tourism can suffer (as a result of algal blooms and vector-borne diseases in new areas), and there can be losses of food exports (e.g., cholera and seafood) and other commercial activities. Diseases occurring across taxa (agriculture and livestock) ultimately threaten the development of all societies, north and south.

CONCLUSION AND RECOMMENDATIONS

Growing microorganism resistance to antibiotics and the resistance of pests to pesticides highlight the need for better understanding of the environmental reservoirs and factors influencing these emerging infectious diseases.

Disease outbreaks may be seen as signals that ecosystems are losing resilience and resistance; perturbed by social, ecological, and climate change, they are giving way to rapidly proliferating, opportunistic r-selected species. These biological "side effects" of overloaded biogeochemical cycles, unlike the direct health impacts of chemicals, have the potential of increasing exponentially.

There are several levels of strategies to confront this threat:

1. Health surveillance must be reinforced. The infectious disease programs and laboratory capacities of CDC and WHO have actually *lost* capacity during the past decade.

2. Health surveillance must be integrated with environmental and climatological monitoring to provide early warning systems and timely public health interventions.

3. Policies on land use, development, and energy must be approached in terms of vulnerability to climate factors and disease. Escalating carbon emissions are having, and will continue to have, profound impacts on the earth's biota, where habitats and relationships among species have evolved and established themselves over millions of years.

Greater energy efficiency in transport and industry is required. And, ultimately, humankind must learn to mimic photosynthesis, the process that began 3.8 billion years ago, when cyanobacteria—the first chlorophyllic bacteria—learned to seize the sun's energy, catapult and capture electrons stepwise, split H_2O molecules, store energy, and release O_2 (oxygen) and O_3 (ozone).

Changing the way humans convert energy is fundamental to avoid exhausting our living (e.g., timber) and fossil (e.g., coal, oil, gas) resources and generating wastes at levels beyond the recycling capacity of natural biogeochemical systems.

Changes in climate, agricultural patterns, migration, and other environmental factors are inextricably linked to health, specifically to trends in infectious diseases. Seminar participants concluded that the area of environmental health and justice, generally given little if any attention by health professionals, must be an integral component of nursing education, research, and practice. A timely report recently published by the Institute of Medicine (IOM), *Nursing, Health and the Environment* (Pope, Snyder, and Mood 1995), provides an extensive review of the current status of environmental health content within nursing, and is recommended for review and implementation within the profession.

With regard to the nursing role in emerging infections, a population-based, epidemiological approach to the education of health professionals (O'Neil 1993) will be vital, and session participants have recommended that such a systems approach be increasingly prominent in nursing curricula. It was also recommended that the Academy help interpret and disseminate information on emerging infections within the nursing community.

Another conclusion from the session was that any attempts to prevent or control emerging infections must involve all health care disciplines and the public. The strong association between lower socioeconomic status and educational levels with the increased incidence of infectious diseases (enhanced vulnerability in rural and urban settings) highlights the importance of strong public health measures and infrastructure. There are many instances in which infectious diseases thought to be on the wane (e.g., syphilis, TB, measles) have experienced resurgences when public health programs such as immunizations or surveillance and resources were reduced or withdrawn (Office of Disease Prevention and CDC 1993).

A mandate for nursing must include a role in public education and strong and effective advocacy for public health infrastructure. Recommendations promulgated at the AAN meeting stressed the need for the Academy to collaborate with other groups who are also supporting global public health strategies and to endorse more active involvement of nursing in the science literacy education of children and adolescents so that the public can better interpret information it receives from a variety of sources.

Session participants acknowledged that prevention is of primary importance with regard to emerging microbial disease since many infections are not treatable. Even for potentially treatable infections, the costs of treatment usually outweigh the costs of prevention (CDC 1995). This is an area in which the nursing profession should take a major lead, and the emerging infections group emphasized this in its recommendations.

Recommendations regarding the control of emerging infections have been published recently by several groups, most notably CDC (1994), the Committee on International Science, Engineering, and Technology (CISET) of the President's National Science and Technology Council (1995), and the IOM (Lederberg 1992). The session participants endorsed these recommendations, which are summarized in Table 2 in four categories: surveillance, prevention and control, applied research, and infrastructure. Recommendations for the nursing community and the AAN which resulted from the 1995 meeting are listed in the final column.

Table 1. Examples of Emerging Infectious Diseases/Agents

Ebola hemorrhagic fever

Escherichia coli 0157:H7

Hantavirus pulmonary syndrome

Human immunodeficiency virus

Lassa fever

Legionnaires' disease

Lyme disease

Rift Valley fever

Ross Valley fever

Vibrio cholerae 0139

Dengue fever and Dengue hemorrhagic fever

Malaria

Leptospirosis

Cryptosporidiosis

Table 2. Recommendations / Goals Related to Emerging Infections

I. Surveillance

CDC	CISET	IOM	NURSING/AAN
• Strengthen notifiable disease surveillance at state and local levels. • Establish two physician-based Sentinel Surveillance Networks. • Establish four population-based Emerging Infection Epidemiology and Prevention Centers. • Strengthen and link four existing sites for a global consortium.	• Establish regional disease surveillance and response networks. • Develop a global alert system. • Assist WHO in establishing global surveillance of antibiotic resistance and drug use.	• Coordinate international infectious disease surveillance for United States through CDC. • Promote development and implementation of a comprehensive global infectious disease surveillance system, with the United States taking the lead.	• Support, interpret, and disseminate to the nursing community recommendations made by other leading agencies (e.g., CDC, CISET, IOM), focusing on implications for nursing.

II. Prevention and Control

CDC	CISET	IOM	NURSING/AAN
• Develop additional means to deliver laboratory and public health information informing health professionals about emerging infections and antimicrobial drug resistance. • Develop and implement guidelines for prevention of opportunistic infections in immuno suppressed persons.	• Encourage and assist other countries in making infectious disease detection and control a national priority. • Preserve existing U.S. government activities that enhance other countries abilities to prevent and control emerging health threats. • Work with private and public sectors to improve United States capacity for emergency production of diagnostic tests, drugs, and vaccines.	• Introduce measures to ensure availability and usefulness of antimicrobials and to prevent emergence of resistance. • Develop and implement through EPA alternative, expedited procedures for licensing pesticides.	• Collaborate with other professions and policy making groups in mutual support, endorsement, and evaluation of global strategies to prevent/reduce the threat of emerging microbial diseases. • Communicate with other nursing groups, recommending that they develop and disseminate to their own constituencies policies and standards to prevent the spread of emerging infections. • Identify mechanisms to promote appropriate prescription and use of antimicrobial agents. • Address strategies to enhance host resistance and immune competence. • Take leadership in major initiatives to focus on preventive strategies. • Take an active role in science literacy of students grades K-12.

III. Applied Research

CDC	CISET	IOM	NURSING/AAN
• Reestablish extramural program to support emerging infectious disease prevention and control activities. • Initiate prevention effectiveness studies to assess impact of food preparation guidelines.		• Develop a comprehensive computerized infectious disease database through the U.S. Public Health Service. • Expand and coordinate NIH - supported research on agent, hospital, vector, and environmental factors that lead to infectious disease emergence. • Increase research on surveillance and control; costs and benefits of prevention, control and treatment; diagnostic tests. • Increase priority given by NIH to personal and community health practices relevant to disease transmission.	• Promote in nursing education and curricula a population-based, epidemiological, system approach for nursing practice and research.

IV. Infrastructure

CDC	CISET	IOM	NURSING/AAN
• Provide state-of-the-art training in diagnosis and testing for laboratory personnel. • Establish a public health laboratory fellowship.	• Ensure reliable lines of communication between local and national medical centers and between national and international reference facilities. • Identify regional and international resources to provide diagnostic reagents for low incidence diseases. • Identify and strengthen WHO Collaborating Centers. • Establish authority of US government agencies to make most of effective use of their expertise to build worldwide surveillance and response network. • Enhance collaboration between US agencies. • Rebuild US infectious disease surveillance infrastructure.	• Develop and implement strategies to strengthen state and federal efforts in U.S. surveillance. • Allocate additional resources to CDC to enhance the National Nosocomial Infections Surveillance System (NNIS). • Expand CDC's Epidemic Intelligence Service and Field Epidemiology Training Program. • Continued support of Dept. of Defense overseas infectious disease laboratories. • Congress consider legislation to fund a program for training in public health and related disciplines. • U.S. develop a means for generating stockpiles of vaccines and a "surge" capacity for vaccine development and production. • Priority and funding be afforded to develop pesticides and other measures to press vector-borne diseases.	• Serve as a clear voice among policy makers for support of public health advocating support for public education, public health infrastructure, and policies which protect the environment and promote ecological balance.

AAN =American Academy of Nursing
CDC=Centers for Disease Control and Prevention
CISET=Committee on International Science, Engineering, and Technology
IOM=Institute of Medicine

REFERENCES

Centers for Disease Control and Prevention (CDC). 1994. Addressing emerging infectious disease threats: *A prevention strategy for the United States*. Atlanta: the Author.

•••. 1995 (June 9). Costs of core public health functions. *Morbidity and Mortality Weekly Report* 44: 426-428.

Garrett, L. 1994. *The coming plague*. New York: Farrar, Straus and Giroux.

Jouan, A., Coulibaly, I., Adam, F., et al. 1989. Analytic study of a Rift Valley Fever epidemic. *Res Virol* 140:175-186.

Kunin, C. M. 1993. Resistance to antimicrobial drugs—A worldwide calamity. *Annals of Internal Medicine* 118: 557-559.

Lederberg, J., Shope, R. E., Oaks, S. C., eds. 1992. *Emerging infections: Microbial threats to health in the United States*. Washington, DC: Institute of Medicine, National Academy of Press.

Moran, G. J., Kyriacou, D. N., Newdow, M. A., and Talan, D. A. 1995. Emergency department sentinel surveillance for emerging infectious diseases. *Annual of Emergency Medicine* 26: 351-354.

Morse, S. S. 1995. Factors in the emergence of infectious diseases. *Emerging Infectious Diseases* 1(1).

National Science and Technology Council (NSTC). 1995. *Report of the NSTC Committee on International Science, Engineering, and Technology (CISET). Working group on emerging and reemerging infectious diseases*. Washington, D.C.: the Author.

Office of Disease Prevention and Health Promotion and Centers for Disease Control and Prevention, Prevention Effectiveness Activity. 1993. *For a healthy nation: Returns on investment in public health*. Washington, D.C.: U.S. Department of Health and Human Service, Public Health Service.

O'Neil, E. H. 1993. *Health professions education for the future: Schools in service to the nation*. San Francisco: Pew Health Professions Commission.

Pope, A. N., Snyder, M. A., and Mood, L H., eds. 1995. *Nursing, health, and the environment*. Washington, D.C.: National Academy Press.

Shope, R. E., and Evans, A. S. 1993. Assessing geographic and transport factors and recognition of new viruses. In *Emerging viruses*, S. S. Morse, ed. Oxford: Oxford University Press.

Spratt, B. G. 1993. Resistance to antibiotics mediated by target alterations. *Science* 264: 388-393.

Summary and Recommendations

from the American Academy of Nursing
1995 Annual Meeting and Conference,
Health Care in Times of Global Transitions

Recommendations regarding actions and directions were presented to conference attendees during the morning session of the closing day. The majority of these were addressed to the Academy and its members but some also included other interested parties and the concerned world at large. Rapporteurs from each of the conference sessions presented a summary of their respective sessions' discussions and the recommendations for action that their sessions' participants had agreed upon.

The Academy thanks the rapporteurs for their comprehensive and thought-provoking reports and all session participants for their very constructive and helpful input.

HEALTH CARE IN TIMES OF GLOBAL TRANSITIONS: PRESENT AND FUTURE (ROGER WINTER)

1. Educate the community about the role of the nursing and medical professions in responding to refugees.

2. Establish a foreign affairs working group.

3. Reorient the United Nations toward stronger protection of the rights and aspirations of people and away from its emphasis on the rights of sovereign member states.

4. Apply those international human rights laws and treaties we have when governments "go bad."

5. Develop a way to respond more adequately to the protection and assistance needs of internally displaced people.

6. Understand and defend the right of asylum.

7. Uphold the ethnic and racial diversity here in the United States and make it work.

IMMIGRATION AND DIVERSITY:IMPLICATIONS
FOR HEALTH AND ILLNESS

1. Put mechanisms in place to protect women and girl children refugees against sexual violence, exploitation, and discrimination and protect their access to food and assistance.

> a. Give refugees themselves the support and the means to improve this protection.

> b. Give women a role in the design and determination of camp location, camp operations, and the workings of assistance programs.

2. Ensure the delivery of reproductive health care to pregnant women, adolescent girls, single or non-childbearing women, and elderly women, stressing preventive care.

> a. Include maternal care, family planning, HIV/AIDS and STD prevention, education, and treatment.

WOMEN ACROSS THE LIFE SPAN

1. Database development: Use for descriptions of communities and for building policy and legislative agendas. Include particular emphasis on the identification of community assets.

2. Establish community partnerships: Advocate adoption of primary health care as a framework around which communities and health care professionals can develop a holistic model of health care. This model includes partnership between public and private groups—including grassroots organizations, business, and the for-profit health provider community.

3. Ensure collaboration within nursing : Strengthen cooperation and coordination among AAN, ANA, and ICN in working with governments and health officials regarding matters of migration, international humanitarian aid, and refugee issues.

4. Pursue legislative advocacy and action on behalf of women.

5. Advocate mechanisms to ensure that people can communicate about their health concerns in their preferred language.

EMERGING MICROBES
Education

1. Support, interpret, and disseminate to the nursing community recommendations made by leading agencies (e.g., CDC, IOM, CISET) concerning the spread of emerging infections, focusing on the implications for nursing.

2. Promote in nursing education and curricula a population-based, epidemiological systems approach for nursing practice and research.

3. Take an active role in ensuring science literacy among K-12 students.

Prevention: The academy should take leadership in major initiatives to focus on preventive strategies for infection including:

4. address strategies to enhance host resistance and immune competence.

5. identify mechanisms to promote appropriate prescription and use of antimicrobial agents.

6. serve as a clear voice among policy makers of support for public health, advocating support for public education, public health infrastructure, and policies that protect the environment and promote ecological balance.Collaboration

7. The academy should communicate their position about emerging infections to other nursing groups, recommending that they develop and disseminate to their own constituencies policies, recommendations, and standards to prevent the spread of emerging infections.

8. Collaborate with other professionals and policy making groups in supporting, endorsing, and evaluating global strategies to reduce the threat and prevent the spread of emerging microbial diseases.

OLDER POPULATIONS

1. Reaffirm the achievement of *Healthy People 2000* goals. Use these goals as quality controls, regulations, and standards for agencies.

    a. Target groups would include HCFA, HMOs, WHO, Blues, and HCAs.

    b. Look at sources of funding using fund evaluation research and outcome research, and conduct research on elders concerning the achievement of the goals of *Healthy People 2000*.

    c. Advocate community agencies-implementing *Healthy People 2000* goals.

2. Facilitate healthy self-care behaviors and attitudes in elders. Help elders differentiate between culture-based self-care behaviors which promote their health and those which may be detrimental to their health.

3. Encourage the development of alternatives to long-term care. Advocate increasing access and decreasing the eligibility requirements for nursing home care. Encourage community-based culturally consistent care.

4. Promote the realization necessary among some groups (e.g., accrediting bodies, surveyors, attorneys) that elder persons value self-determination over safety.

5. Advocate the abolition of government regulations that penalize older working persons.

6. Recognize that the concept of retirement has different meanings and implications among different countries, different cultures, and for persons from different socioeconomic levels.

7. Investigate and publish information about restrictions on elders who undergo mandatory retirement.

INTERNATIONAL HUMANITARIAN LAW

1. Prepare a cadre of nurses skilled in national and international armed conflict situations.

    a. Prepare and use short-term courses.

    b. Use faculty with international experience in armed conflict situations.

    c. Develop a directory of nurses with experience in armed conflict and/or humanitarian relief.

    d. Possible collaborating organizations include ICN, ANA, the ANA International Nursing Center, NCIH, the International Red Cross, and the Federation of Red Cross and Red Crescent Societies.

2. Include in nursing school curricula courses on armed conflict, humanitarian law, human rights law, and values and ethics.

    a. Include the history of nursing and armed conflict situations.

    b. Emphasize nurses–responsibilities to provide care for those on both sides of armed conflict.

    c. Teach alternative models of conflict resolution.

    d. Include narrative from nurses who have worked in armed conflict situations.

    e. Discuss U.S. social and economic issues that could lead to local conflicts.

    f. Discuss the implications of international humanitarian law policies on how nursing does research.

    g. Develop a core curricula encompassing the points above within the context of a discussion of the right of access to food and water.

3. AAN expert panels on international nursing and ethics should develop and disseminate position papers concerning:

    a. opposition to violence.

    b. discrimination and violence against women during armed conflict.

    c. children as active participants in violence.

    d. banning land mines.

CHILDREN

1. Advocate health care and immigration policies that support the integrity and unity of the family.

2. Promote the position vis-a-vis legislation and health policy that every child is entitled to accessible health care.

3. Recommend research to develop and test innovative, theory-based, culturally sensitive systems of care that promote the health and development of vulnerable children and their families.

4. Support efforts to broaden nursing education to include an international health care focus and the politics of health care.

5. Promote research on the subjective experience of upheaval (e.g., immigration, home-lessness) for children and its impact on health.

6. Recommend research to identify and test culturally sensitive, developmentally appropriate, measurable outcomes related to the health of vulnerable children and their families.

7. Foster collaborative partnerships with children and their families, community groups, other disciplines, and potential funding sources to design, conduct, and disseminate research that focuses on the health of vulnerable children.

NOTES

NOTES